GEEL REVISITED
After centuries of mental rehabilitation

| Acknowledgements |

The authors wish to thank the foster families, clients and numerous members of staff who participated in this study. This book is dedicated to them. It could not have been written without their generosity and both their knowledge and experience which they were more than happy to share with us. Thanks to Dr Jef Wouters, Medical Director, for supporting this research project. We are very obliged to Wilfried Bogaerts, rehabilitation psychologist, and Dr Lode Weyns, rehabilitation psychiatrist: their comments during the final stages of the book were a tremendous help.Thanks to Dr Alex Cohen, Harvard Medical School, who joined Roosens in Geel for two months of research in the year 2000 and did background research in the States. We are most grateful to Woestijnvis and in particular Arnout Hauben, producer and director of the film 'Geel' respectively, for joining our efforts to propagate the story of Geel. And finally, thanks to Meri Hitchins who subjected this book to the scrutiny of a native speaker and especially to both our families for their patience and support while we were working on this book.

Eugeen Roosens & Lieve Van de Walle

Geel Revisited

After centuries of mental rehabilitation

Foreword by Oliver Sacks, M.D.

Garant

Antwerpen-Apeldoorn

Eugeen Roosens & Lieve Van de Walle
Geel Revisited
After centuries of mental rehabilitation
Antwerp – Apeldoorn
Garant
2007

129 pp – 24 cm
D/2006/5779/118
ISBN 978-90-441-2075-2
NUR 772

Cover design: Koloriet
Cover painting: Maarten Mangelschots

Garant
Somersstraat 13-15, 2018 Antwerp (Belgium)
Koninginnelaan 96, 7315 EB Apeldoorn (The Netherlands)
Garant/Coronet Books, 311 Bainbridge Street Philadelphia PA 19147 (USA)
Garant/Central Books, 99 Wallis Road, London E9 5LN (England)
www.garant-uitgevers.be uitgeverij@garant.be
www.garant-uitgevers.nl info@garant-uitgevers.nl

Contents

About the authors

Eugeen Roosens

Eugeen E. ROOSENS, Ph.D. (°1934) is Emeritus Ordinary Professor (Anthropology) at the Katholieke Universiteit Leuven and Emeritus Extraordinary Professor at the Université catholique de Louvain. He started his career at Leuven in 1966, after studies at the Katholieke Universiteit Leuven (Ph.D.) and short doctoral study periods at Oxford, Harvard and the Sorbonne. E. Roosens is the author of numerous articles and books. E. Roosens was a visiting professor at Universities in the United States (UC Berkeley, eight times), Canada (Laval and Montreal), and Japan (Nanzan). He was appointed the P.P. Rubens Professor at the University of California at Berkeley for the academic year 1989-1990. He did fieldwork in the Congo (1961-1965), in Quebec (eight periods between 1968 and 1999) and in Geel, Belgium (1971-1975, 1999-2000, 2005-2006). Since 1974 through 1996 he was in charge of the project "The Cultural Identity of Ethnic Minorities", a long-term fieldwork project of a team of scholars which operated on five continents. E. Roosens held the National Francqui Chair ("Master classes") at the Vrije Universiteit Brussel for the academic year 1996-97.

Lieve Van de Walle

Lieve Van de Walle (°1963) is a linguist by training. She studied at the Universities of Ghent and Antwerp, was awarded a fellowship by the FWO and was research assistant at the University of Illinois at Urbana Champaign (Illinois, US). She obtained a PhD in Linguistics from the University of Antwerp. Having taught English and various communication related subjects at several colleges and universities, she currently works as the manager of the Rehabilitation Programme at the OPZ in Geel.

As an anthropologist Roosens conducted all the fieldwork reported in this book. Van de Walle only got involved when the cases were being written up and translated. Hence, whenever "I" or "we" is used in relation to the cases discussed, it exclusively refers to Roosens. All other chapters, bar the ones on the history of the foster care programme (chapter I) and its tradition (chapter V), are a joint effort.

Foreword

Geel is a unique social experiment—if one can use the word "experiment" for something that arose in so natural and spontaneous a fashion. In the seventh century, the daughter of an Irish king fled to Geel to avoid the incestuous embrace of her father, and he, in a murderous rage, had her beheaded. Well before the thirteenth century, she was worshipped as the patron saint of the mad, and her shrine soon attracted mentally ill people from all over Europe. Seven hundred years ago, the families in this little Flemish town opened their homes and hearts to the mentally ill—and they have been doing so ever since.

When a family, often a couple with young children, indicates its readiness to take in a boarder (and at one point numerous families in Geel had at least one boarder), they are given no information, and make no inquiry, about their guest's psychiatric condition or diagnosis. The guests are brought into the home as individuals, and integrated into family life in every way: they live with the family, eat with the family, go out with the family. When the relationship works well, as it does most of the time, the guests become cherished family members, like a beloved aunt or uncle. They may play a part in bringing up the children, and grandchildren, or in taking care of the elders.

The eminent anthropologist Eugeen Roosens has studied this unique community in depth for over thirty years, and first published his observations in 1979 (*Mental Patients in Town Life: Geel: Europe's First Therapeutic Community*, Sage Publications). Now, with his collaborator, Lieve Van de Walle, he has produced an even more remarkable book, *Geel Revisited.* Like his first book, this is based on minute and continuing research which is both objective and warmly human and sympathetic, and the writing is both rigorous and accessible, with a charm and flavor all its own (like the town itself). Roosens and Van de Walle start by providing a short history of the seven-hundred year project of community life in Geel, a most detailed and fascinating consideration, focussing especially on the radical ways in which Geel has developed in the last century and a half.

There has always been controversy about how "disturbed" or "eccentric" people should be treated, probably since the dawn of civilization. Should they be treated as ill, possibly dangerous, confined in institutions? Or is there a chance that a more human and social approach, trying to reintegrate them into family and community life, a life of love and work, will succeed as well? At the beginning of the nineteenth century, when Pinel struck off the chains which had been used for centuries to shackle mad people, and a humane breath swept over Europe, this question was epitomized by Geel. Could a place like Geel provide a real alternative?

As Roosens and Van de Walle write, the Geel solution is "not simply a happy but isolated remnant of the Middle Ages." The system there has undergone at least two fundamental transformations which have allowed it to remain viable. The first occurred when the Belgian government introduced medical supervision in the community, and built a hospital there which was finished by 1861. Here, if things got too difficult for the family to handle, a boarder could go for medical treatment. Thus fortified by a hospital and professional staff—

psychiatrists, nurses, social workers and therapists—providing both family and (if need be) medical care, Geel continued to flourish, at one time before World War II hosting several thousand mentally ill boarders.

And a second change, in the last forty years, has occurred as the impact of health professionals in Geel has markedly increased. During the day, over half of the patients are able to take part in jobs or day programs, away from home, supervised by therapists and social workers. (Intentionally or not, this rise in day-care situations has coincided with a decline in home-based work, as more and more of the host families have moved into non-agricultural jobs.)

Thus, as the authors write, Geel has evolved into a "two-layered system," but a number of key elements of the traditional system have remained intact: "maximal kin-like inclusion and integration of the patient, the kindness of the broader social context in Geel, the acceptance of the patients' inherent limitations, the strong bond between boarders and foster families, the resilient mutual loyalty, and the entrenched responsibility of the next generation towards the boarders."

When I visited the town recently, I saw guests strolling or bicycling in the streets, chatting, working in shops. I would not have known that they were boarders (apart from the occasional odd mannerisms or behaviours), except that my hosts, from the hospital, were able to identify them for me. In the world at large, the mentally ill are often isolated, stigmatized, shunned, feared, seen as less than fully human. But here, in this little enclave of Geel, it seemed to me, they were respected as fellow beings, treated with affection and care—at least as much as anyone else.

When I asked several foster families why they had welcomed such a guest, they seemed confused. Why would they not? Their parents and grandparents had all done the same; here it is a way of life. The people of Geel may know that their neighbor, say, is a guest, with mental problems of one sort or another—but such a fact lends, seemingly, no stigma. It is simply a fact of life, unremarkable, just as being male or female would be.

"For the residents of Geel," the authors write, "the line between 'patients' and ordinary people is, in many ways, nonexistent. The prejudices against mental illness that are very much alive in the world at large are not found in the people of Geel, because they have been raised, for many generations, in the presence of mental 'patients.'"

"What makes Geel remarkable," the authors conclude, "is not the blurring of the boundary between normal and abnormal, but the recognition of each patient's human dignity, to the extent that, for them, family and community life is given an honest chance every single day."

While Professor Roosens has done fieldwork in the Congo and elsewhere, and taught in universities all over the world, his second home and heart have remained in Geel, where he is at once a deeply respected member of the community and a most acute observer of it. His colleague, Van de Walle, is likewise a part of the fabric of life in Geel, as the manager of Geel's psychiatric hospital. They are thus able to provide, as no one else could, nineteen detailed portraits of families and their boarders, some of whom Roosens has observed over a span of decades. These families and their guests present a wide range of situations, from benign and almost romantically happy situations in which the hosts and guests love and care for each other deeply, to other homes in which the guests are “difficult” (Geelians speak of “good” boarders or, more rarely, “difficult” ones, but never of “bad” or “crazy” boarders)—so difficult that the fostering situation has broken down. Even where very severe psychiatric problems exist, Roosens points out, when “a mutual warm relationship evolves [as it usually does], foster parents are prepared to go to great lengths to accommodate their guests.”

These nineteen case studies are exemplary in their richness and detail, and constitute primary material of enormous value. Along with the rest of the book, they provide a definitive rebuttal of the notion of mental illness as a remorselessly advancing and deteriorating condition and shows how, if there can be an effective integration into family and community life (and, behind this, a safety net of hospital care, professionals, and medication where warranted), even those who would seem to be incurably afflicted can, potentially, live full, dignified, loved and secure lives. *Geel Revisited* should be required reading for anyone interested in community care or the treatment of those with mental illness.

Oliver Sacks, M.D.

Introduction

Geel (pop. 34,000) is well known throughout Flanders, the northern part of Belgium. *Van Dale*, the main Dutch-language dictionary, lists under the word *Geel*: "expression: *bound to go to Geel, to come from Geel*: to be mentally ill." In other words, in popular discourse Geel is associated with mental illness and the care for the mentally ill. Traffic signs all over Geel signal "Family Care", urging people to adjust their speed and drive carefully. That mentally ill people live with "normal" families and go as they please generally stuns outsiders. The latter clearly feel uncomfortable with the mentally ill and resort to humour when addressing the issue. "Half-Geel is entirely crazy; and entire Geel is half-crazy," is a popular saying one often hears in neighbouring villages. Throughout Flanders the word "Geel" elicits a broad, amused, or even cynical smile, especially among people who have never visited the place.

The image of Geel in the rest of the world is in sharp contrast with this Flemish stereotype. In professional circles abroad, Geel is virtually considered a monument of mankind, a unique institution (Bachrach 2000). Over the years, lots of psychiatrists, psychologists, health managers and politicians from numerous countries have visited Geel, looking for firsthand information. There have been visitors from as far a field as Australia, Brazil, Thailand, Japan and China. In 2000, more than 300 professionals from various countries attended an international congress on Geel, held in celebration of its 700th anniversary. In 2005, 500 professionals participated in the *International Congress on Balanced Care*. Geel was mentioned as best practice in the 2002 WHO report, *Mental Health, New Understanding, New Hope*. CBS made a short film on Geel for its blockbuster programme *60 Minutes* (March 31, 2002) and thus introduced Geel to roughly 11 million people worldwide. In 2003, the psychiatrist Raj Persaud dedicated an entire episode of the programme *Travels of the Mind* to Geel. It was aired on BBC World Service.

As Geel's system of community care has organically grown over seven hundred years and is firmly ingrained in the entire population, it is not all that surprising it generates interest worldwide. As early as the 13th century, mentally ill and retarded people came to Geel, imploring Saint Dimpna for assistance. By the middle of the 19th century, Geel had become a state institution, a "colony" for the mentally ill. From then on, medicine, especially "psychological medicine", expanded fast and started to play an important role. In the 1850s and 1860s, any self-respecting scholar in the field of psychiatry visited Geel and formed his personal opinion on the system. "The Geel Question" was born. It basically divided the psychiatric community into scholars "pro" and "contra" Geel. The issue wasn't settled until 1902, when, at the *International Congress of Psychiatry* in Antwerp, a large majority proclaimed Geel as best practice to be reproduced wherever and whenever possible. Between 1850 and 1940 foster care spectacularly expanded, but after World War II it entered a period of steady decline. The modernization and industrialization of the region considerably affected the system. Small-scale agriculture made way for industry. In most families both partners started working outside the home (cf. further analysis in *Chapter II*).

Despite the falling numbers, it is fair to say that the foster families, assisted by a highly motivated team and management, are as resilient as ever and go about their business as usual.

They feel personally responsible for their boarders and are convinced the system will endure. While interviewing 108 foster families, in 1999-2000 and in 2005-2006, we never had the impression we were confronted with a system that was petering out. This does not mean older foster parents are not aware that "the younger generation is not committed in the way they once were."

New elements may influence the course of history, however. After years of steady decline, accelerated by a passive attitude by the then management and red tape by the government, the OPZ finally woke up in the late 1990s. The new management immediately set up a think-tank to study and contain the serious problems the foster programme faced. Using more active forms of recruitment, the current administration has recently attracted both young families and new clients. It looks like the efforts are paying off. Foster parents, currently enjoying the status of partners, are very supportive of the system. Moreover, referring bodies, like general practitioners and mental health centers, seem to positively respond to the OPZ's active and more assertive approach. Media are allowed in, so a broader public is informed about the system. Modern communication strategies are in place. It is up to the politicians and the Department of Health and Social Welfare now to throw the system a life-line.

Of course, nobody can predict the future, and that is not the aim of this book. What we do want to achieve is to draw a well-documented, realistic and graphic picture of life in foster families at the onset of the 21st century. In our modest opinion, a critical and reliable description is badly needed. Since the publication of Eugeen Roosens' first book on the subject in 1979 (cf. *References)* no comprehensive study on Geel has been made. In the period 1970-1975, Roosens visited more than 100 families, while three research associates interviewed all families twice (1,000 in those days). As this first anthropological study was only one part of the ambitious *Geel Project* sponsored by Columbia University and the University of Louvain, anthropologists were asked to limit their scope, and focus on the patients' interactions within the wider community, *outside* the family context: on the streets, in the churches, the cafés, the cinema and other public places. This first Geel book was published in five languages, including Japanese (Roosens 1977, 1979a, 1979b, 1982 and 1983).

Twenty-five years later, encouraged by Harvard Medical School, Roosens embarked on a second research project, *Geel revisited.* The study started in 1999, proceeded in 2000 (Roosens 2001), and was resumed in 2005 and 2006. In contrast with the previous book, the current study is more encompassing and broader in scope. It primarily focuses on the families, and more specifically on how they perceive their role as foster parents. *Chapters IV* and *V* form the nucleus of the book. In these chapters the families' own quotes and reference frames are used as a point of departure. The cases *(Chapter IV)* give as graphic a sketch as possible of the rich diversity of situations and types of relationship—illustrating the patients' participation in "real life". No patient is like the other, no family is like the other, hence, the gallery of sketches. Irrespective of this diversity and obvious "chaos", the authors did manage to identify recurring patterns. As outlined in *Chapter V*, a therapeutic tradition does seem to exist, traditional know-how that is handed over from one generation to the next. These chapters are preceded by a few chapters that sketch the broader context of psychiatric family care. The book starts with a historical overview and zooms in on the "Geel Question". In *Chapter II* it dwells on the changes that have occurred in the system since the previous book was published. In *Chapter III* it is explained how the psychiatric foster care programme fits in the larger organization and how the programme is run on a day-to-day basis. Last but not least, throughout the book psychiatric foster care is situated within the larger framework of community care. Basically, the book tries to establish the past and future potential of psychiatric foster care as a form of balanced community care and aims to highlight the value of fostering for the mentally ill with enduring psychiatric disabilities.

In December 1999, 549 patients were living in 455 foster families. Some families hosted two or three (the maximum) patients. With the approval of the board and the management, we asked the 12 district nurses to each select 9 families: 3 among the oldest families, 3 among the youngest, and 3 middle-aged families. The total was 108. This study, although not strictly representative, does reflect the huge diversity of the foster families in Geel. In 2005-2006 we revisited 19 carefully selected families. Our method and research techniques conform to the rules of ethnography. In this sense, the study wants to make a contribution to the field of medical ethnography. We try to represent as closely as possible how foster families have been communicating about themselves and their relations with present and former patients. Keeping in mind that we, as researchers, are part of the picture, we summarize their exposés, while adding data collected from other sources[1]. Out of respect for the privacy of the clients, medical files were not consulted. As foster families do not use "learned" descriptions or classifications, we did not need this sort of information anyway. However, for the professional reader we present a brief overview of the main diagnostic categories *(DSM-IV)*. Reference date is 30 June 2006:

N=460		
Disorders Usually First Diagnosed in Infancy, Childhood or Adolescence	*99*	*21.6%*
Delirium, Dementia and Amnestic and Other Cognitive Disorders	*2*	
Mental Disorders Due to a General Medical Condition	*6*	
Substance-Related Disorders	*12*	
Schizophrenia and Other Psychotic Disorders	*112*	*24.4%*
Mood Disorders	*51*	*11%*
Anxiety Disorders	*24*	
Somatoform Disorders	*16*	
Dissociative Disorders	*1*	
Sexual Disorders and Gender Identity Disorders	*5*	
Eating Disorders	*2*	
Impulse-Control Disorders	*55*	*12%*
Adjustment Disorders	*5*	
Personality Disorders	*4*	
Other Conditions That May Be a Focus of Clinical Attention	*60*	*13.1%*
Additional Codes	*5*	

1 We draw on internal documents, professional publications and unpublished materials about the history of Geel, and more than 50 interviews with members of staff at all levels: with the General Manager, Business Unit Manager, the Medical Director, all psychiatrists and generalists; nurses, social workers, and the staff in the workshops and district centres.

| Chapter I |
A short history of psychiatric foster care in Geel

Origin and religious dimension

This chapter sketches the rich heritage of the Foster Family Care Programme in Geel. In addition, it gives an overview of the wealth of scientific studies published in various languages over the past 200 years. Our research draws on three types of sources. First, publications in Dutch by a few prolific and highly professional members of the Geel Historical Society and the *Geel Project* (De Bont 1976, 1989; Eynikel 1971a and 1971b; Koyen 1973; Veraghtert 1969, 1971, 1972, 1975, 1976). Secondly, a number of scientific articles written in English and published in medical journals. These were traced by Dr Alex Cohen of Harvard Medical School, in the Harvard libraries. Most of them appeared in the middle of the 19th century, at the time when the "Geel tradition" was taken over by the state and put under medical control. Thirdly, unpublished reports kept in private collections, books and articles in both Dutch and French. As far as we know, a synthesis drawing on all these sources has never been written before. The overview stops at about 1970. *Chapter II* picks up where this chapter leaves off.

Since its beginnings in the 13th century, the "Geel tradition" has gone through several major transformations. Geel's psychiatric family care can be traced back to the legend of Saint Dimpna, an Irish royal princess supposed to have fled her father around 600 AD, fearing the latter's incestuous intentions. Dimpna ended up in Zammel, a hamlet of Geel, where she was overtaken and captured by her father who then had her beheaded near Saint Martin's chapel. Before long, so the story goes, Dimpna was invoked in people's prayers to cure various illnesses, especially insanity, as her father was deemed to have acted in a bout of insanity. As Dimpna, by her heroic death, had withstood the devil that had entered the mind of her father, she was allegedly able to expel all evil spirits. And as in these days most illnesses, including mental ones, were blamed on evil spirits, Dimpna became the patron of an exorcising cult. The first historic traces of her rituals go back to the 13th century. In the year 2000, foster family care celebrated its 700th birthday.

In 1349, the first stone of Saint Dimpna church was laid and about a century later a "sick room" was built next to the church. Those seen as possessed or mad resided in the church during religious penitence rituals which took nine days to complete (novena). Pretty soon, however, the sick room was too small to accommodate all pilgrims. Awaiting a vacancy, patients were placed in the care of local Geel families. In addition, not everyone returned home after the rituals, so the number of foster families increased as time went by. Originally, only people living in the immediate vicinity of the Saint Dimpna church fostered patients, but from the 17th century onwards the mentally ill were also housed in other districts in Geel. Foster parents received financial compensation in return for their services. Clerics used to organize the pilgrimages, took care of the rituals, allocated foster homes, supervised the care in the families and had spiritual jurisdiction over all the pilgrims.

Initially, Dimpna was invoked to cure all sorts of diseases, but as time went by her scope narrowed to the field of mental deficiencies. That was the very simple beginning of the now famous "boarding families" (*kostgevers* in Dutch), and their "boarders" or "guests" (m.: *kostgasten*, f.: *kostmensen*). These terms persist in the Flemish dialect spoken by most of the local villagers to this very day. Terms like "foster families" *(pleeggezinnen)*, "patients" *(patiënten)*, and "Public Mental Hospital" *(Openbaar Psychiatrisch Ziekenhuis)* weren't introduced until fairly recently. They are a clear signal of the professionalisation which has taken hold of the system over the past few decades. In colloquial language, both sets of words are now used interchangeably.

At present, the Christian name Dimpna is still widespread in the Geel population. Moreover, everybody knows the Saint Dimpna church, remembers the Dimpna cult, and is aware of the Dimpna procession every five years. This is about the extent of Dimpna's influence in this day and age, though. The religious beliefs, rites and miracles are a thing of the past. To those of us familiar with contemporary Geel it was almost shocking to see an American participant invoke Saint Dimpna during a session at the Geel Conference in 2000. She implored the Saint to illuminate US politicians' minds and begged them to take to heart the homeless mentally ill. We all realised that this prayer was not a religious act as such, but it was an unusual happening to say the least, a voice from a distant past. It certainly wasn't a part of the world we live in today, a world in which Dimpna has been basically relegated to folklore. Secularization is very strong in "Catholic" Flanders; less than 12% goes to church on Sundays. In the discourse of most educated people, Catholics included, saints, performing miracles, belong to the realm of myth and magic.

It is, of course, hard to determine exactly how important the religious dimension of the system has been over time. What we do know for sure is that the cult of Saint Dimpna and the pilgrimages by the mentally ill existed as early as the 13th century. We also know that foster care was supervised by the local chapter of canons, the "Catholic establishment", until the end of the 18th century. Geel still prides itself on its epithet of "Merciful Town". Even so, it is unlikely that only charity and mercy have driven the resilience of the Geel tradition. Trustworthy historians are adamant, that the economic dimension played a significant role throughout its history. The sudden boom in the middle of the 17th century is principally due to financial considerations: officials in charge in Flemish villages, towns and cities sent their penniless mentally ill *en masse* to Geel. The Geel solution was a lot cheaper than locking them up in institutions. The influence of the clerics came to an end after the French invasion in 1797. Consequently, the chapter was abolished. This doesn't mean the tradition grinded to a halt, however. On the contrary, in order to cut expenses the city of Brussels closed its asylum in 1803 and brought all of its 100 patients to Geel. Many other cities followed suit. As a consequence the number of boarders rose exponentially over the next few decades. It went up from 200 in the year 1800 to 400 in 1820. It was at 900 in 1850, the year the spectacular international expansion took off. It needs to be said that the living conditions of the patients in those days were not comparable to what they are today. The "sick" mostly lived with small peasants, whose houses were plain and basic, uncomfortable by today's standards, certainly. Hygiene was below par, even by rural 19th-century standards.

In the course of the 18th century, new ideas on the care for the insane emerged and signalled the end of the age-old hagio-therapeutic treatment. In spite of these developments, the family care system in Geel survived, be it without the ritual component. It was supervised by the local municipality until the Ministry of Justice took over in 1850. In 1850, Belgian Parliament decided to tackle the situation of the mentally ill and passed the *Law on the Mentally Ill*. Geel became a "colony" and was put under the supervision of the Minister of Justice. In 1851 further regulations were issued, outlining the administrative structure and medical guidelines. In 1861 an infirmary was built as temporary accommodation for the mentally ill who first arrived in Geel and for those who needed medical assistance for shorter periods of time. This countered the main criticism that severely mentally ill patients were left in the care of families without proper medical attention. In the law the church's role was reduced to a bare minimum, and although the appointment of a Catholic chaplain was scheduled as early as 1851, it didn't take place until 1892. Clearly, religious rites had taken a backseat. Some religious aspects did survive, however. Saint Dimpna's procession was held every single year until the 1970s, when the clergy deemed this tradition "too mythological" and cancelled the event. At the time of the *Geel Project* in 1971-1975, dozens of foster parents criticized the clergy's decision. Not that they believed in the healing power of Saint Dimpna; they just felt that the procession was part of their joint heritage so it didn't feel right to abandon it. The tradition was picked up again after heavy protest from the local population. To this day the procession takes place every fifth year. Older foster parents mentioned that they used to go on pilgrimage to Saint Dimpna's chapel in Zammel with their parents, although they were quick to add that they no longer did so (Roosens 1979a). Als already mentioned, in 1971 through 1975, our research team conducted over 2,000 interviews, and in 2000 we personally interviewed more than 100 families; not once was Saint Dimpna mentioned as a source of healing.

The curate of Saint Dimpna's, who was in charge of the cult, told me in the early 70s that the stream of native pilgrims had completely dried up, but that letters and donations sent by US citizens were still coming in. Most of these letters were very moving personal requests. They expressed deep belief and implored the intervention of the Saint, mostly on behalf of a son or daughter. Some letters constituted a series written by the same person, a tragic testimonial of the steady decline in the person's mental state.

To sum up, it is crystal clear to all parties involved, that mental illnesses and deficiencies have nothing whatsoever to do with the devil or other evil spirits. Miraculous healing is a thing of the past.

Dramatic expansion

Karel Veraghtert, one of the historians collaborating in the *Geel Project*, attributes the boom which occurred between 1850-1940 to the important and steady improvement of the patients' material and medical conditions due to the *Law on the Mentally Ill* and the establishment of the Infirmary. Both measures guaranteed access to medical services and basic living conditions. In all fairness, however, Geel's expansion had started well before1850.

As early as the 17th century the number of patients started increasing as Geel rose to fame. Although the Duchy of Brabant remained its most important catchment area, there were quite a few patients from the coastal areas and the southern parts of Wallonia too. They even came from as far a field as the Netherlands, Germany and France. According to Koyen's extensive and detailed article (1973), the places of origin at the beginning of the 17th century were the following:

Antwerp: 112	*'s Hertogenbosch: 14 (NL)*	*Brecht: 8*
Mechelen: 58	*Rozendaal: 13 (NL)*	*Mol: 8*
Brussel: 26	*Kasterlee: 12*	*Tilburg: 8 (NL)*
Turnhout: 25	*Eindhoven: 11 (NL)*	*Berlaar: 7*
Diest: 14	*Breda: 10 (NL)*	*Ekeren: 7*
Herentals: 14	*Oosterhout: 10*	*Hoogstraten: 7*
Lier: 13	*Louvain: 9*	*Baarle-Hertog: 7 (NL)*
Hasselt: 6	*Aarschot: 8*	*Schijndel: 7 (NL)*
Tongeren: 6	*Lokeren: 6*	*Zundert: 7 (NL)*
Retie: 13	*Ghent: 5*	*Bergen-op-Zoom: 5 (NL)*

As De Bont, quoted by Veraghtert (1976: 499) demonstrated, Geel increasingly developed into a European project between 1850 and 1940. In 1860, Geel counted about 800 patients. All nine provinces were represented: Antwerp 152; Brabant 291; Hainaut 29; Limburg 33; Liège 53; Luxemburg 27; Namur 31; Eastern Flanders 55, and Western Flanders 5. They were joined by foreigners: Germany 5; England 4; France 9; the Netherlands 71; other countries 37. And that was just the beginning. Between 1915 and 1935 the number of foreign guests peaked: the Netherlands 255, France 47, Germany 7, other Western-European countries 13, Eastern-European countries 6. Geel even hosted a few US, Japanese and Brazilian guests. In those days, several Dutch mental hospitals were overcrowded and sent their patients to Geel. In 1923, 421 Dutch resided in Geel. Most of them paid their own way and expected services of better quality. Quite a few stayed with the local upper class. Geel also inspired other countries to set up a psychiatric foster care programme. In all, there were 174 initiatives spread over different countries, some of which, direct or indirect copies of the Geel system (Eynikel 1971a, Godemont 2000: 13). In 1884, Lierneux, a town situated in the Province of Liège, set up a foster care programme to accommodate French-speaking patients. Lierneux still exists today and hosts about 110 patients. French-speaking patients continued to come to Geel, though, regardless of linguistic and cultural differences. Some Geelian families were even keen on taking in French-speaking boarders. They hoped that their children would pick up a second language. Usually, this did not work out, as most French-speaking patients quickly switched to the local dialect.

In 1882, a Dutch centre, the "van Dissel Circle", was founded by Reverend van Dissel in order to "nourish" and stimulate the religious, cultural and social life of the Dutch boarders. The "van Dissel House", located at the town centre, later opened its doors to all patients and became a successful social club. It used to attract more than 150 patients every Sunday, until December 1999, when it was closed because it no longer met fire regulations. The present social club, which was opened in 2001 and was named the *"Statie"* as it is located close to the train station, is still referred to as the *"van Disselhuis"*. The name refers to the concept of the social club rather than to the building as such, and is yet another clear sign that Geel and its inhabitants do not easily absorb changes. Older foster parents still remember the times when a multitude of foreigners lived in Geel.

By 1900, about 2,000 patients resided in the village. That number rose to a staggering 3,736 in 1938. During World War II figures dwindled. They fell to 2,600 in 1944. Only 34 Dutch guests remained, 19 French, 2 Germans, and 7 boarders coming from other Western-European countries. The figure for Eastern Europe remained at 6. Part of the explanation is that the Dutch had expanded their own capacity in the meantime, establishing new mental hospitals. Since prices in Holland were now lower than in Geel, Dutch patients were rushed back home. In the early 1970s about 1,300 boarders were present in the community. In 2000 this number was at 550 and, on 30 June 2006, it was at 460. The post-war catchment area is Flanders. In 1975, 4 new patients originated from Geel, 27 from the rest of the county of Turnhout, 8 from the rest of the Province of Antwerp, 8 from the rest of Flanders, and 5 from the rest of Belgium. One patient arrived from the US (Veraghtert 1976: 500) (for recent statistics cf. *Chapter II*).

"The Geel Question"

This passage, is based upon articles and books by 19th-century medical doctors, both Belgian and international. Most of the historical sources used are to be found either in the OPZ Archives and Library or in the Harvard University libraries. As for the latter I was assisted by Dr Alex Cohen of Harvard Medical School. In the period 1840-1870 Geel was visited by a number of medical doctors-specialists, generally referred to as "alienists". They introduced Geel to the international scientific scene. The questions they were most interested in were whether the system was based on sound practice and was thus worth exporting, and whether the system was more efficient and humane than the "modern" asylums of their day. All sources concur on the fact that Esquirol played an important role in giving Geel a platform (cf. Sibbald 1861: 32 and Duval 1867). Esquirol visited Geel as early as 1821, which resulted in an article published in 1822. Ten years later he referred to Geel again in one of his popular books. Around 1840 the illustrious professor Guislain from Ghent visited and assessed Geel. His advise, by the way, was negative (Duval 1867). But it wasn't until the French ex-colonial and publicist Jules Duval—a complete outsider—published an article, that Geel was brought to the attention of the international community. In 1867 Duval published a comprehensive and richly documented study on Geel, *Geel ou une colonie d'aliénés (Geel or a colony for the alienated)*. Duval was an ardent defender of the Geel system.

Dr Parigot too, the Colony's first medical director, played an important role in the promotion of Geel. The same goes for Dr Bulckens, his successor, who was in close contact with the royal family. The Belgian Royals were in favour of the Geel System with its caring families, its freedom and its clean and healthy air, and they said so too. Dr Jaromir, Baron of Mundy, a doctor originating from Moravia, advocated Geel's cause in several countries with almost missionary zeal (De Bont 1989).

De Bont (1989) wrote a short but well documented history of the national and international discussion concerning the "Geel Question" as the controversy was referred to in the years

1840-1870. What we will try to do here is to zoom in on the exchanges between professionals about the alleged therapeutic and medical value of the Geel System, and about the question whether this approach can be copied elsewhere.

Reading Duval's book and some 60 articles published in the period 1840-1870, it struck us how often researchers' views were skewed by emotional and moral arguments. Most commentators are either totally pro or contra Geel. Only a small number of professionals present a more balanced picture. Even 19th-century experts observed this. Loiseau, notes in 1862:

> *Numerous articles have been published, be it independently or in several proceedings in France and abroad with two things in mind, first, to present a detailed analysis of this truly exceptional village, and, second, to determine both its value and its downsides. Some have praised it to the skies, others have completely slated it* (Loiseau 1862a, translated from French).

Most medics, involved in this debate, either contributed to the establishment of big, modern hospitals or were employed by one. In their perception these modern hospitals were the very incarnation of the innovative approach as launched and propagated by Pinel at the onset of the 19th century: people with mental problems should no longer be treated as outcasts or prisoners but as sick people. Medics who visited Geel were well aware of the fact that the scientific basis for treating severe psychiatric illnesses was embryonic at best in those days, but these "alienists" or specialists firmly believed in psychiatric science all the same. They were absolutely convinced of the progress of their profession and its potential to produce valuable remedies. To them, a system like the one in Geel where patients were handed over to the illiterate, to peasants and small tradesmen seemed an aberration. One of the visitors, the French Dr Falret, writes in his 1861 report:

> [...] *we cannot believe that the very foundation of our science would be ill-conceived and that one would have to claim—like the ones who advocate Geel—that fresh air and freedom basically suffice to treat the alienated* (Loiseau 1862a, translated from French).

This rather sceptical appreciation of the Geel system and the way it operated prior to 1850, when medical supervision had not been put into place by the Belgian government yet, seemed widespread in those days. We noted a radical reaction by the French Dr Ferrus, who visited Geel in the 1840s. He thought Geel was a bad idea, from whichever angle you looked at it. But what he most objected to was that one did not give treatment to the mentally ill; and that, he thought, was morally unacceptable. Even after a medical team had been installed in Geel, Ferrus did not change his mind. He thought Geel was the pits:

> *One happened to quote the Colony of Geel as an example in that discussion. I for one believe that it is impossible to do something that is equally despicable. For the "alienated" treatment and freedom cannot go hand in hand. In Geel there is no treatment, and the alienated have nothing but freedom which is harmful to them* (as quoted in Duval 1867: 186-187, translated from French).

Dr W. Browne, a Scottish expert, was not exactly mild either in his judgement about the Geel system:

> *It afforded the last glimpse of a mediaeval condition, incrusted with the stains and corruption of a worn-out organization, where the faith in the supernatural had faded away, and the sun of science had not yet arisen* [...] (Parigot 1863).

In our view, similar judgements are not based on objective facts but essentially on impressions. Other medics too give a free rein to their emotions rather than form a rational opinion. Some are cynical about the so-called freedom one enjoys in Geel and refer to the twenty or so people running around handcuffed in the streets of Geel, or those that are shackled in their foster parents' homes. That hundreds of psychiatric patients did move about freely was a fact they chose to ignore.

These critics are of the opinion that the community of Geel is one immense asylum, since most inhabitants keep an eye on the mentally ill. And maybe, the critics continue—but they failed to investigate this hypothesis—there are quite a few ill people who cannot even enjoy this fake freedom because they are locked up in themselves. Such patients might even be as happy in a closed institution. And how does one explain, their argument continues, that patients regularly attempt to escape from Geel? The "board givers" are in charge of preventing flight and are reprimanded when it does occur. If the mentally ill feel so free in Geel, they wonder, why escape at all? Then the above measure would be quite unnecessary too.

Dr Loiseau writes in this regard:

> *At Geel, where there are a large number of incurables, there are many patients of that class who are happy, but who would be the same in this respect in an asylum, since they do not appreciate the blessing of liberty nor feel its value* (Loiseau 1862b).
>
> [...] *In fact, at Geel the lunatic is far from enjoying the same amount of liberty as the other inhabitants. Because he is a patient, he forms a part of the population which excites in the rest a kindly pity, and on account of which he receives the right of protection which is constantly exercised towards the lunatic by the mere effect of the superiority of reason over folly. This general surveillance, exercised at all times by the sane population upon the insane, is not one of the least attractions of Geel for the attentive observer* (Loiseau 1862b).

Even so, these negative observations are countered by the following passage:

> *At the present time, and with the prejudices existing in all classes against the insane, and with the apprehension, to a certain extent legitimate, which the insane inspire in all those around them, one cannot hope to realise in another country the extraordinary phenomenon presented at Geel of 400 insane persons moving freely about in the midst of a population which tolerates them without fear and without emotion* (Loiseau 1862b).

A fraction of the visiting doctors insinuated that there was almost certainly hidden sexual abuse in a village where male and female patients were free to mingle, and that some foster fathers would not be able to resist the temptation. That would certainly be the case in France, it was argued, if one were to establish a colony of this type:

> *Moral values and habits significantly differ between Flanders and France. Consult the statistics and you will find in the annual crime review that the Justice Department reports a 53% increase in acts of indecency. And would you entrust hysterical women to people who only think about money, and who are only driven by self-interest. Moreover, one wondered whether it wasn't harmful to the inhabitants' mental health. One was particularly concerned about the children who lived with mentally ill people and shared the intimacy of their own home* (*Discussion sur la colonisation des aliénés* 1862, translated from French).

Apart from these semi-subjective considerations, some hard facts contra the Geel system were brought forward. Several visiting doctors observed that hygiene in many houses was problematic. A number of detailed accounts were given. The farther one was removed from the centre of town where the situation was usually more favourable, the worse it got. Prior to the time when state inspections took place, i.e., prior to 1850, one found patients sleeping in very small rooms that were difficult to air. Some patients shared a bed with members of the family. Linen wasn't always clean. In cases where patients were incontinent or dirtied themselves in other ways, it was not a pretty sight.

Dr Carmichael McIntosh captures the situation as follows:

> *As regards the hygiene of Geel and its neighbourhood, the state of filth everywhere abundant, except, perhaps, in the central street, gives one no very exalted opinion. Assuredly in no British village, with half the interest attached to it, would such a state of things be permitted. Stinking ditches, collections of manure, putrid pools, &c., abounded in the outskirts and back dwellings of the town. I saw a good many cases of skin disease of the face and mouth in the young children playing about the roads, and this is not to be wondered at. From the before-mentioned report, we learn that during the four years—1856, 7, 8 and 9, smallpox, cholera, influenza, dysentery, and typhoid fever, have reigned epidemic at Geel* (Carmichael McIntosh 1862).

In the guest houses one did not have a bath-tub and it was impossible to take care of a patient's hygiene. Poorer families were struggling to provide decent meals. The meals were simple and there was little variation.

Yet another rational medical observation ran as follows: It is completely impractical to spread mentally ill patients, some of whom need the control, support and medical attention of a doctor, over so extended a territory. Geel is one of the largest towns in Belgium. The distances are so big and the number of patients living wide apart so numerous, that the provision of medical care is virtually impossible. Medically speaking, the geographic spread of patients is nonsense. The four doctors who work at the Colony are not in a position to follow up on hundreds of patients, even if the majority of the mentally ill do not need daily or even weekly care. Inevitably, Geel is a system where only the most urgent cases or crises are brought to the attention of a doctor. The others, the majority of the patients, are never reached.

In 1852, A. Brierre de Boismont reported on a visit that took place in 1846, and he described the situation in Geel prior to the establishment of the medical services:

> *Nothing has been done about physical and moral treatment. One does not have baths, one has no facilities to deal with crises, no infirmary to cope with incidental illnesses, and consequentially there is no central pharmacy. Those alienated who flee, those who misbehave, those who steal or try to commit suicide, arson or murder are shackled. This is barbaric and often harmful to these unfortunate people as they might develop bruises and ulcers due to the shackles* (Brierre de Boismont 1852, translated from French).

The above observations are worded in a milder form by another visiting doctor, Dr J. Sibbald:

> *The mistake of sending unsuitable cases for treatment is, to my mind, the most fruitful cause of the present defects of Geel. Demented patients, of dirty habits, form a considerable proportion of the population, and, from what I saw, I have no doubt of the impropriety of subjecting them to the cottage treatment* (Sibbald 1861).

The patients' physical well-being could not be guaranteed due to the geographical spread, it was thought. For doctors who were convinced of their profession's positive impact, the argument presented below by Dr Falret in his 1861 report makes perfect sense:

> *The most important downside of Geel, the one that, in our opinion, beats all the others and balances out all its advantages single-handedly, is the placement of the alienated amongst peasant families, spread over a vast area. This is the very negation of every idea of active and individual therapy, be it physically or morally* (Loiseau 1862a, translated from French).

However, one does also find lots of testimonials and passionate pleas that ardently defended the Geel system. Nearly all visitors, even the most critical ones, were convinced that the patients were socially integrated to a large extent, if not fully, in their foster families. There was never any debate about that. The advocates interpreted this level of inclusion of the mentally ill as a clear sign of compassion, civilized behaviour and extraordinary charity. They also felt that a similar positive approach must have a benign effect on the sick and have a healing effect. Visitors who spent the most time in Geel or who worked in Geel for an extended period all concurred that it is the matter-of-fact way people in Geel deal and live with the mentally ill that makes it so exceptional.

Duval writes:

> *The freedom, the work, the distractions are only fully realized in the environment specific to Geel, i.e., family life; and that, in all honesty, is the ultimate characteristic that distinguishes this Belgian community from all counterfeits established by the authorities* (Duval 1867: 62, translated from French).

One can qualify this argument as rational in the sense that in Geel one does offer severely mentally handicapped people almost complete access to the intimacy of family life. How patients, and in particular different types of patients, experience this level of integration and what the effect is on their psychiatric condition still needs to be established, in our view. In order to determine the effect on the mind of this social integration one needs closer analysis, case by case. We do understand why opponents consider the claim that social inclusion must have a healing effect as romantic and "idealizing", as something put forward by the faint-hearted proponents. But social inclusion in the family in itself is a hard fact. Undeniably so.

Outspoken as they are, the proponents of the Geel system with its freedom, work, family life and fresh air, speak out against the large asylums. The modern, luxurious asylum, in their view, may look like a palace, but it feels like a prison. People are locked up; they are surrounded by lots of companions with similar problems who have a negative influence on one another. Their life is conditioned by a clock or a drum. Patients realize all too well that they got robbed of their freedom. Everyday social life in a family, a village, a neighbourhood is a distant dream only. The sick are closely watched and guarded by supervisors. There is no such thing as an open sky, even the courtyards are surrounded by walls. Decline is the only way to go. Mostly, proponents of the Geel system do not expect much of the medical profession, a sentiment which truly offends some opponents and leads to some snide comments:

> *If Dr. Parigot calls the medical officers of asylums dreamers, psychologists, and mad doctors, and praises St. Dymphna, if he represents the asylums as prisons, and speaks of liberty and non-restraint in Geel, where the sick people are put in "fetters, chains and irons," he will no doubt produce the most disadvantageous impression upon your countrymen, who have established the best asylums of the world, and who are the last to be deceived by sophisms* (Willers Jessen 1860).

As one can read below, Dr Parigot was not blinded by Geel as is implied in the above quote:

> *The principal communes which had patients there, sent to Geel a representative, whose duty it was to overlook the lunatics who were lodged and clad by the commune he represented. Brussels elected Dr. Parigot to perform this function for its lunatics. At the time of these appointments, Dr. Parigot tells us that the administration of the colony was in the saddest confusion, and that the position of lunatics was perhaps even more cruel than that of the Negroes he had seen in South America* (Foreign psychological literature 1860).

When addressing the issue of asylums, Duval is fairly radical in his judgement and tends to generalize:

> *The love for passive order, present with the entrepreneurs or directors of institutions, will always make them feel contented with satisfying appearances, resulting from the application of rules; and these rules, even those that are deemed very wise, will have the inevitable shortcoming that they submit a large number of sick who are totally different in their health and sanity alike, to invariable and identical*

> *discipline. Within this official and inflexible framework, one's personality is trembling, gets irritated or wanes, and with it a moral and powerful leverage in the healing process disappears* (Duval 1867: 99-100, translated from French).

Roughly ten visiting doctors are more nuanced in their judgement. They underscore that a system like the one in Geel, as any other system, has its pros and cons. The advantages Geel undeniably offers are social integration in the family and local community, the opportunity to work, and its fresh air; to take part in all sorts of social activities and to develop one's remaining capabilities and skills. Geelians are convinced that there are normal dimensions in every single patient that one can build on or that can be maintained. The easygoing relationship between Geelians and patients is largely due to the fact that lots of Geelians grew up amongst patients.

Dr J. Moreau (de Tours), medical doctor of the hospice de Bicêtre, writes in 1845, a few years before the central medical services were established in Geel:

> *In a colony, like the one in Geel, the crazy people are not merely elevated to the dignity of the sick, as Esquirol so beautifully puts it, they have not completely lost their dignity as reasonable human beings; for they have not completely broken with society, to which they remain linked by all the aspects of their intelligence that the illness has left unscathed* (Moreau 1845, translated from French).

Even so, this very same author, a true advocate of Geel, is not blind to the faults of the system in its pre-medical days:

> *Geel was nothing more than a depot, a sort of Botany Bay, a place where Belgium sent its 'alienated' who, having undergone a short treatment in some hospice or other, had gotten labelled incurable. They were forgotten there and only those that got better and were conscious of their recovery, re-entered society by themselves* (Moreau 1845, translated from French).

> [...] *Serious forms of abuse got established. The management of more than 700 alienated was, so to speak, random. Even the administrative and medical reporting was negligent; the alienated were placed in the community and left again 'healed' without the authorities being informed. One did not bother about the necessary authorisation. Families did not obtain any information at all about the ill. And even if one had seriously wanted to make an effort to treat the patients, it was entirely impossible. The colony was a vast field of observations, uncultivated and sterile for science* (Moreau 1845, translated from French).

And yet, Dr Moreau's appreciation for the Geel system overrides the negative aspects:

> *To them, treating the insane, meant to simply live with them, share with them their work, their distractions, as far as this was psychologically possible, and even though this sort of treatment might be the most efficient of all treatments from a scientific point of view, it was carried out too without giving it much thought, because*

> *those that put it into practice didn't even think of informing the public about it, just like they did not consider teaching the public to work its fields and raise its families, and so on* (Moreau 1845, translated from French).

The protagonists of Geel also emphasize the love of the insane for the children of the family and the positive response of the children involved (Carmichael McIntosh 1862). They argue that simple family life comprises curative processes that put people who have gone astray on the right track, to some extent at least, if not completely. And if this doesn't take place for whatever reason, at least the patient gets offered a humane atmosphere, totally lacking in an institution. In that sense one can understand that the advocates of Geel are more inclined to put their money on the traditional, non-professional practice rather than on the contemporary medical-psychological science. Looking at things from this angle, the geographical spread of patients was a minor issue as the alleged benefit of medical science was minimal at best.

As for that issue, Dr Sibbald noted in 1861:

> *The dissimilarity of the mode of life in an asylum from that to which they have been previously accustomed, and the appearance of their habitation—part palace, part barrack, part prison, in some instances surrounded with a high boundary wall—all combine to impress such minds with sensations of so injurious a nature, that the removal of these impressions forms an important element in the details of asylum management. To be boarded in a cottage with a family of his own rank of life, joining in the family meals, to watch the amusements or the employments of the children, to take a part in the various incidents of home life, with the probability of having healthy affections and emotions excited by the social relations between himself and his new friends, and to mix little with any who would be likely to encourage feelings of discontent, would afford to such cases all advantages which the most benevolent philanthropy could devise* (Sibbald 1861).

And:

> *One of the agreeable features of the place is the general contentment manifested by the insane. In very few cases, indeed, did they complain of the injustice of their detention, though questioned on the subject. The comparative liberty, or "free air", as M. Parigot terms it, was evidently valued by them as a great privilege, more especially among those who had been previously resident in asylums* (Sibbald 1861).

Dr Sibbald recognizes in Geel rehabilitation *avant la lettre*:

> *Nearly all those who have visited Geel have recognised to a greater or less extent that it possesses many advantages. It has at least taught us that the reform begun by Pinel and Tuke is not yet complete; that though insanity has been raised from the degradation of a crime to the rank of a disease, the afflicted victim is still treated too much as if he were a prisoner; though the fetters which disgraced humanity have been struck off, there is still much to be done before the sufferers will be raised to that social standing which many are both able and worthy to occupy* (Sibbald 1861).

From this perspective, the spread of patients over a large territory is even beneficial. Due to the spread, one distances patients from a hoard of unfortunates suffering from the same or a similar condition. As opposed to hospitals, Geel managed to normalize the environment.

J. Webster holds a passionate plea for the preservation of Geel but suggests a number of improvements:

> [...] *an opinion exists in some influential quarters that, instead of still further improving the colony of Geel, it ought to be entirely broken up and discontinued. In short, the insane inmates should henceforward be consigned to public asylums, shut up within four stone walls, only associate together, and never be allowed to enjoy the society of their own fellow-men, until they also have become victims of mental derangement. No greater and more disastrous mistake could be committed, than to carry out such an absurd proposition. Correct abuses; still further improve internal discipline; remunerate the medical staff more liberally; make the communes pay higher allowances for their pauper patients, so as to ensure increased comforts to such sufferers; supply additional means towards promoting trades and manual employments amongst men, as also work for women; and lastly, but still not the least essential, forthwith establish an infirmary both for the temporary reception of acute cases, and of those inmates who may become attacked by physical disease. Doing these things effectually, in my opinion, would be the most proper course to pursue—not, certainly, by adopting any thoughtless scheme of destruction* (Webster 1857).

The faction that put forward Geel as an example of a humane and efficient approach finally got the upper hand at the international conference *(Congrès International de l'Assistance des Aliénés et spécialement de leur Assistance Familiale)* held in Antwerp, September 1902. In the conference proceedings, *Rapports et compte-rendu des séances* (Sano 1903), we read:

> *The president articulates Professor Tamburini's wish which seems the most general and gets the most sympathy. The entire assembly supports Professor Tamburini's wish. Nobody contests it, this wish clearly captures the general sentiment on the fundamental issue that was the main subject of the debates* (Sano 1903: 859, translated from French).

The conclusion, proposed by Tamburini and approved by the conference, went as follows:

> *The conference expresses its wish that family care would be applied in all its forms as widely as possible* (Sano 1903: 859, translated from French).

This leads us to the conclusion that as early as 1860-1870 Geel "rehabilitated" its patients, to resort to a term that is now commonly used in psychiatric circles after forty years of deinstitutionalization (Lamb and Bachrach 2001; van Weeghel et al. 2005).

In addition, one needs to say that the Geel system has always been exceptionally cheap, too cheap possibly. Several 19th-century authors pointed this out. A few visiting scholars even calculated that most foster families could not manage with the fees they received. Webster noted in this respect:

> *But, however cheap food and lodging may still prove in "Kempen-land," the actual profit must be nil, out of nine pounds ten shillings sterling; after feeding, clothing, and lodging an adult lunatic boarder. Undoubtedly, in many instances, their labour is given besides, but not invariably; and, although industrious working inmates are more in request than idle patients, parties must take their chance, with reference to such contingencies* (Webster 1857).

This sounds remarkably familiar to the debate that is presently preoccupying the OPZ management. The programme runs a huge deficit; the contribution paid by the authorities does not nearly cover the ever increasing expenses (cf. *Chapter III*).

What is amazing is that the debates that took place in the middle of the 19th century are so similar to today's. Things change fast, but then again, they don't.

| Chapter II |
Recent developments and strategy for the future

Patients blend in

From a purely material point of view patients are far better off than 25 years ago. A significant change for the better is that patients are properly dressed. Some buy their own clothes; others are assisted by their foster parents or the district nurse. The wellness centre[2] helps them look after their personal hygiene. It is harder to tell them apart from other citizens. Only those patients with striking physical features are easy to identify. In former times, well remembered by the older foster parents, "the guys of the Colony" were poorly dressed. Fabrics of low quality and little imagination were used, and foster mothers had to repair threadbare garments over and over again. A first improvement came some 50 years ago when the OPZ opened its own clothes store. It stayed in business until the 90s, when it was closed down. Some foster mothers regretted this as the store offered excellent services and functioned as a one-stop shop where one could purchase all one needed. The vast majority of foster parents and their guests, however, are delighted with the present arrangement. Most foster mothers we visited take pride in their boarders' good appearance. They buy them the best clothes they can afford. Some foster families even sponsor their boarders. Foster mothers tend to keep an eye on their choice of colours, and the way they combine pieces. They want to make sure they are dressed in good taste. Some do not entirely trust the shopkeepers and prevent the latter to take advantage of their foster son or daughter.

It is safe to conclude patients' living conditions and social and psychological well-being have considerably improved over the years. Many older foster parents even use the words "immensely improved". "Patients have all their heart desires; they have become true ladies and gentlemen!", one of my interviewees proclaimed. I am certain that this statement was heartfelt and made without a trace of envy.

Medical assistance

Today's medication has vastly improved people's quality of life. While in the early 1970s patients and their foster families were reluctant to use medication, in 2000 they truly appreciate what medication can achieve. Both parties see it as a major step forward, as it prevents major depression or psychotic crises, fits, deviant behaviour in public places, etc. Painful

2 There is a wellness centre in one of the district centres. In the centre, patients can bathe under the supervision or with the help of nurses and certain preventive measures are taken, e.g., monitoring of weight and blood pressure. Flue shots are administered, wounds are dressed, etc. Most patients go there at least once a week. There is also a hairdresser and a pedicure. Afterwards, patients can go for a drink in the café.

confrontations in which nurses or bystanders have to physically fight patients to keep them under control are a thing of the past. Even so, psychiatrists in the foster care programme choose not to take centre stage. In his address at the 2005 Congress (Van de Walle 2005), Dr Weyns, the OPZ's current rehabilitation psychiatrist, argued that "the psychiatric professionals should keep a low profile and adopt a 'serving' attitude. Their ultimate goal should be to make themselves increasingly superfluous." The level of medical assistance provided in Geel is in line with what rehabilitation literature recommends: good access to psychiatric care without it being a domineering factor in people's lives. People need to get on with their life, take responsibility for their own recovery rather than heavily lean on the medical profession.

Money liberates

Most boarders enjoy a state pension of some sort; nobody is penniless or left at the mercy of others. The benefits aren't generous but they cover the basic needs. Often, a legal guardian is appointed by the judicial authorities to manage the patient's money and business affairs. In those cases the OPZ social worker functions as go-between. A few patients look after their own money; they are assisted by their district nurse or foster parents if necessary. All other patients receive pocket money so they can buy small treats such as cigarettes, sweets, meals, drinks, etc. They can offer their mates a drink or treat their beloved. They can buy the members of their family gifts, bring souvenirs from their trips or they can throw a party, e.g., on the 25th anniversary of their arrival in the foster family. Most can afford to travel once a year and can participate in sports or leisure activities. If they work at the OPZ, fortnightly, they receive a small salary which they are free to spend as they wish. In case they can afford it, patients acquire a radio, television or bicycle, or whatever they want. Some patients are true collectors; one for instance is the proud owner of hundreds of CDs (cf. *Chapter IV,* case 2).

Some patients run a small enterprise and are keen traders. One patient, for instance, breeds rabbits and sells them on the market. Another charges horrendous prices for cigarettes. Those who are not permitted to smoke and aren't too clever about money eagerly purchase them. Another boarder daily brings extra sandwiches from his foster family's kitchen and sells them to colleagues with a large appetite. Yet another collects money on New Year's Eve. Some patients are thrifty, they would rather die than spend money and manage to save significant sums. Now and then, boarders decide to leave their estate to their foster parents; in that case they have their will registered at a notary's office. From the 108 families we visited, we met several boarders who had been doing exactly that. The OPZ social workers keep a close eye on patients' finances and make sure nothing untoward happens in that respect.

Social integration in contemporary Geel

Due to their increased "invisibility", patients are free to visit any café or restaurant in the town centre. Although cafés and restaurants have recently moved up-market, which reflects the increased wealth of the community, patients are still welcome. Often, foster parents take their foster son or daughter out for dinner or drinks. Sometimes it is the other way around, and it is the patient that treats his foster family. There is only one establishment in the cen-

Bicycle repair shop: work offers both status and structure to the day
(Photo OPZ)

tre of Geel that is not open to “guests”; even so quite a few “invisible” guests are served without any fuss. This doesn’t mean, of course, there is no stigma attached to being mentally ill at all. Some patients in our sample are very aware of their being stigmatized in one way or another. They try very hard to escape it. Some, for instance, refuse to visit the patients’ social club and do not want to be seen with what they consider the really disturbed or mentally retarded whom they callously refer to as “the loonies”, a term which is taboo in colloquial language. Some of these men and women have friends whom they meet outside Geel on weekends. They might walk by themselves or with carefully selected people. They might also meet with a boyfriend or girlfriend. Some do not want to be associated with the Geel foster care system at all. They see themselves as regular, “normal” foster children who have nothing to do with the mental institution.

Work

Studies have demonstrated the necessity of work for a person to feel whole. Psychiatric patients are no different. Work is crucial as it offers both status and structure to the day. Geelians have always understood that. In the old times, lots of patients were employed by their foster parents. Sometimes people had to work really hard, and there are countless stories about patients being exploited by “wealthy farmers”. These days, Geel is no longer a rural community; very few patients live on farms. And even if they do, there is not a lot of work for them due to mechanization. This explains why about 200 patients daily work in workshops run by the OPZ. That is roughly half of the patient population. Of the people who have recently joined the programme close to 95% gets a job at, or organized by the OPZ. The workshops provide a protective and safe yet stimulating environment, well adjusted to the needs of the clients. Moreover they offer clients social contact and a peer group.

Because patients have very different abilities and wishes and the age span is enormous, the OPZ has developed three basic formulas. On the OPZ campus, there are a number of sheltered workshops that mainly focus on work. It concerns productive activities with economic value. These range from repairing bikes, woodwork, gardening, printing, binding books, running a shop to packaging, assembling, and other types of light industrial work. The occupational therapists take into account the basic interests, skills and wishes of each individual client. So, if people like repetitive work that demands precision, they may be employed in the industrial workshop. If, on the other hand, they like fixing things and are mechanically inclined, the bicycle repair shop is just the thing. Clients do need to commit; once they accept a job in a workshop, it is expected that they come every day and take their work seriously. The aims of the workshops are principally to offer clients structure and to teach them skills as well as a good work ethic. It is important clients can abide by the rules, accept authority, be punctual, concentrate, work in group, solve conflicts, and share.

A second option is supported employment. An occupational therapist is in charge of social relations with employers within the OPZ and in the community. In addition, she screens potential employees, and supports both parties once a contract is in place. The occupational therapist initially coaches the client on the spot and teaches him/her certain skills needed for the job. On the other hand, she paves the way for the client by explaining to his/her fellow workers and supervisor how to handle the client in certain situations. The results so far are very promising. Having made the shift in the 80s and 90s from work in the community to the OPZ's sheltered workshops, the management is now moving back to individual jobs both within the OPZ and the community, be it on a smaller yet more intensive scale.

The third formula is less strenuous and more geared towards clients' general well-being. People daily visit the activity centre in their own district. These local centers provide a mixture of work and leisure. Work is available but not mandatory. People can walk off and do other things, like cook, go for a stroll, participate in creative activities, potter around in the garden, engage in group discussions, read a magazine, etc. The client determines his/her own work rhythm. The occupational therapist supports and stimulates but doesn't control. The main aims are to make one feel at home, to maintain or improve one's skills and to facilitate social contact.

Most patients are well and truly proud of their job. The salary they receive is very small but important, nevertheless. Legally speaking, hospitalized patients cannot perform paid labour, as they are supported by the social security system. Apart from the financial reward, the work gives clients status and a goal in life. In the morning they leave for work just like anybody else. They enjoy their free weekends which they spend as they see fit. Mostly, work is in perfect harmony with life at home.

Leisure

Leisure determines to a large extent one's quality of life. It is also a key to integration and inclusion. That is why the OPZ has heavily invested in the organization of leisure activities over the years: the leisure service offers travel, sports activities and is involved in organizing or participating in events with a cultural dimension. As ordinary people started going abroad on a regular basis, so did the boarders. In the year 2000, 480 patients out of a total of 680 (patients living in the Intramural Facility included) participated. Some groups go to Spain, others to the Belgian coast or somewhere closer to Geel. Some patients also travel with their foster families; a few travel by themselves or with private organizations. To accompany the boarders on their travels, staff members are recruited from the entire Hospital: secretaries, accountants as well as drivers and technicians. The benefit is mutual. Clients meet new people and get away from their daily routine. Staff members get acquainted with a different aspect of the business and meet the boarders. As a consequence, they understand better whom they work for and get a feeling for the family care programme, a bonus indeed. Patients pay for their holidays with their own money. The high ratio of participation suggests that patients are satisfied. In their view, the trip is the event of the year. They generally take lots of pictures, buy loads of souvenirs (especially for the foster parents' grandchildren) and are invariably happy to come home. Some read up on the places they visit, so they arrive well prepared. Food and drink are extremely important to most. As will become apparent from the case studies below, more patients than foster parents travel abroad. Some patients have been to Spain six or seven times, while their foster parents have never left their home, basically. In this sense, patients are more attuned to modern times than their families are.

Sports too are extremely important in boarders' lives. Some of them are amazingly fit and participate in interclub soccer competitions long after they have reached retirement age.

Climbing: working with one's strengths
(Photo OPZ)

Several sports are offered on a weekly basis. Apart from that, people can become a member of the sports club for a fee and this gives them access to all sorts of extra activities: tennis, cycling, walking, soccer, mountain-bike, *pétanque*, "survival", fishing, etc. In 2006, access to regular sports clubs and all sorts of cultural facilities is well under way, but it took a supportive minister and years of hard work and perseverance to get things started. Here too the OPZ has appointed somebody to liaise with local sports clubs and cultural organizations. Sports clubs can get subsidies for setting up a "G-club" within their club. As such the government encourages clubs to include physically and/or mentally handicapped people. These days several OPZ clients play judo, korfball and soccer in G-clubs. It is not much at this point, but it is a start. Another important target for the leisure service is to work on destigmatisation campaigns. The service supports projects with schools, clubs and cultural organizations in both Geel and surrounding communities. These projects mainly have a cultural angle (theatre, photography, arts) and basically aim at integration and inclusion.

Rising costs

Quality has its price. Needless to say, the organization and running of medical, work and leisure services require professional staff and cost a lot of money, money which is well spent as benefits are obvious. Regrettably, the health care authorities do not adequately fund the programme. The OPZ currently receives about €40[3] a day per patient, while the bed-day price in a hospital is currently at €230. On average €18.2 is transferred to the foster parents[4], the OPZ retains the rest to run the programme. Both families and the OPZ are well aware the respective amounts do not nearly cover the costs and energy invested. The OPZ yearly injects a substantial amount of money into its psychiatric foster care programme as it feels responsible for, and takes pride in its heritage. Similarly, foster parents are happy to lay out money for "their Jules" or "Pierre". In the long-term, however, this is not tenable a strategy. As the government continually produces plans to further the cause of community care, and is intent on both reducing cost and increasing efficiency, it would be wise to properly fund a system with international acclaim which has proven its worth. This makes perfect sense from a purely economic point of view.

Social network

Over the last 20 years new types of patient networks have developed. Numerous occasions currently present themselves at which people meet and socialize: holidaying in Belgium or

3 This amount was fixed in 1991 by Royal Decree. Apart from the occasional indexation, it has not been adjusted since. In 1991 the amount represented 75% of a bed-day in an acute ward. Today it has fallen under 20%.

4 A majority of foster parents and staff feel that foster care could be an attractive package, provided that the tax-free allowances for the families are doubled, or at least sharply increased. The idea is that the allowance provides a second income so that one of the partners can afford to stay at home. If one considers that in the county of Turnhout, to which Geel belongs, unemployment is at roughly 10%, one realizes that there is scope for this type of economic activity.

abroad, weekly meetings at the wellness centre, the social club or in the Geel cafés, working at the OPZ workshops, playing sports, etc. Some patients engage in a casual affair; others go steady and have the same partner for years. Sometimes a patient gets accepted as adoptive in-law by the natural family. Emiel, for instance, attended the burial of his partner and was invited to the wake by her next of kin. If we go on the comments made by both patients and their foster parents, most love affairs are not very sexual; they are just "for the company". One feels it is important to have a boyfriend or a girlfriend for social reasons, in order to feel like everybody else. Most foster families joke about the liaisons or so-called liaisons of their guests. Dating among patients started in the 1960s. Before, sexes were strictly segregated. Although most foster parents don't exactly encourage their patients' love life, they do accept that relationships are unavoidable. They would agree that patients need love and affection just like anybody else. There is a general consensus, however, that it would be detrimental to the mental health of their patient if he or she were to go and live together with their partner. According to most foster parents, experience has taught that very few patients, if any, have significantly benefited from erotic or sexual contacts, as was suggested in the years of the "sexual revolution".

Social control

No patient is left to his/her own devices. As is the tradition, district nurses visit foster families unannounced. They rarely make an appointment. So the nurses have a pretty good idea about the way patients are accommodated and treated at home. In addition, most patients often get to meet their district nurse or social worker outside the family home. In case they want to discuss something in private, without their foster parents being present, they can. As mentioned above, about 200 clients are employed in the OPZ workshops; lots play sports, go on excursions or participate in events. As a consequence, should they feel the need, patients can always find people to confide in. And then, there are the infamous gossip networks. Whereas some patients cannot stop praising their foster parents, others constantly complain or find fault with them. This kind of talk is usually taken with a pinch of salt by the OPZ staff. However, when these messages get enforced by others, they will be checked out. During the holidays, when groups of patients accompanied by staff spend a lot of time together away from home, patients tend to compare their situation. It does happen that a patient loses his/her habitual guard and reveals potentially damaging facts. There is always a debriefing after the holidays, so that essential information can be passed on. Geelians in general feel responsible for the well-being of patients and look out for them. In case a patient is readmitted to hospital due to bad treatment by his/her foster family, the family falls into disgrace and is frowned upon, both in their own neighbourhood and in the town at large. Social control has always played an important role. Foster parents also look out for their patients. If they have reason to believe that OPZ employees or fellow patients give their patient a hard time, they will report it. But they will only do so if they are absolutely sure of the facts; they will check and double-check before lodging a complaint. In case families and patients do not feel they are getting anywhere by using the regular channels, they can get in touch with the ombudswoman, a neutral person experienced in handling complaints.

Foster parents are "partners"

There is a general feeling among foster parents that they are held in high regard by the OPZ staff these days. Foster parents are seen as partners, relations are virtually egalitarian. Twice a year foster parents are invited to a meeting where they are given information and can ask questions. Importantly, they are served coffee, tea or other drinks by the very nurses who are their supervisors. During the reorganization process, a representative sample of foster parents took part in focus groups where they could voice their opinion on several topics. Plans exist to establish a council for foster parents. This council will be a sounding board for the management and will be closely involved in the decision-making process. In addition, there is a quarterly magazine to keep foster parents informed. The "policing" days of the authoritarian "section guards", as the district nurses used to be called, are well and truly over. According to foster parents, today's district nurses are kind and well-trained people, who know their job. Last but not least, the present system has reinvented itself over the last few decades to accommodate foster parents' changed lifestyle. Every so often, families want to go away for the weekend or want to travel. In those cases, the OPZ looks after the patients. The latter are either admitted to hospital or stay with another family.

Declining numbers

Although all is well in Geel at first glance, the declining number of patients and foster families and their respective average ages are a cause for serious concern. As already stipulated in *Chapter I*, in the late 1930s the number of patients stood at about 3.700. This number plunged to 992 in 1980, 861 in 1985, 773 in 1990, 525 in 2000 and 460 on 30 June 2006. In recent years the decline has slowed down somewhat. It is hard to predict when or if the number will stabilize. The average age of the patients is currently at 59 and the average age of the foster parents at 64. On 30 June 2006, the oldest patient in a foster family was 93, the youngest 24; the oldest foster parent was 94, the youngest 26. One family has been fostering since 1943, that is 63 years. Traditionally, there have always been more male than female patients (two thirds vs. one third). As for foster parents, the reverse holds: there are 329 foster fathers and 415 foster mothers.

The statistics about the number of patients, alarming as they may sound to the reader who is first confronted with them, are to a large extent a logical consequence of post-war developments in psychiatric care. Psychiatric patients in Belgium used to have but two choices: to be locked up in an institution for life or to come to Geel and enjoy relative freedom. Advances in neuroleptic medicine and psychiatry in general, on the one hand, and more humanitarian and care-oriented policies on the other hand have completely changed the scene. Patients now receive support in their own communities. The assistance offered now ranges from in-patient care, sheltered accommodation and workshops to community mental health teams. People tend to stay near their families or reside in the area they grew up in.

So, psychiatric foster care in Geel has gradually evolved from international to regional care. In the period 2000-2005[5], a total of 89 potential clients were admitted to the programme, i.e. 18 per year on average. A few were brought to Geel by relatives or acquaintances. 31 patients were referred by OPZ psychiatrists during their stay in the OPZ. By far the largest group was referred by 18 different mental hospitals or residential units for the mentally ill (Bogaerts 2006). 75 clients originate from the region (50 km radius of Geel), 14 come from further a field.

As for the decline in numbers of families, the classic explanation runs as follows: Times have changed. On the one hand, young married couples or partners both try to get a well-paid job, social security and pension provisions included, while on the other hand the foster care allowances are extremely low. Moreover, younger generations cherish their privacy and their freedom to move about and travel. The time of the extended farmer families, who could do with a helping hand, is gone. Increasing intolerance vis-à-vis the mentally ill is never mentioned, and according to Roosens, never springs to mind. During the interview sessions, Roosens came across dozens of cases of younger Geelians who had an excellent relationship with their parents' patients, but had decided not to take boarders themselves. "Modern times," then, seems to be the widely accepted explanation. To end on a positive note, so far the Geel programme has never been short of families. New candidates for the *métier* of foster parent still materialize. Recruiting new families is not as easy as it used to be, but it is not insurmountable a problem either. Since 2002 the OPZ has also been recruiting families from the periphery of Geel. This may be part of the explanation why there are still rooms available.

Strategy for the future

The OPZ strategy for the future is to export its particular model of psychiatric foster care and/or know-how to other regions in Flanders and/or other countries rather than to haul all patients to Geel. A small-scale pilot project in the town of Herentals[6] has been initiated. The programme's enormous expansion in the previous century (cf. *Chapter I*) resulted in a solid international reputation which has not faded so far. Of course, this enduring fame is not merely a product of the past. As a wave of deinstitutionalization swept over the globe, lots of experts and professionals came to Geel to watch and learn. Interestingly, some former visitors, like Ellen Baxter, who learned the language and lived with a foster family for the best part of a year, got so inspired she set up a totally different and yet very similar programme in New York. Her target group are the NY homeless, many of whom have mental problems. Baxter's remarkable and highly visible spin-off has grown enormously. In its turn it has deeply impressed and inspired many others. It is hard facts like these that make the Geel project so valuable and worthwhile. New foster care programmes for psychiatric patients have recently been established in several European countries and beyond, as became clear at the *Balanced Care Congress*:

5 By 30 June 2006, 12 new clients had been admitted to the programme. This means that in 2006 the minimum target of 15 admissions a year will be almost certainly met.

6 Town the size of Geel, approximately 20 km from Geel.

> *Psychiatric foster care fits perfectly within the range of community care services. The number of countries establishing psychiatric foster care services is on the rise. [...] In Italy, according to Aluffi (2005), 11 services were active in 2000. In 2005 there were more than 30. In certain regions in Southern Germany about 15% of people with enduring mental health problems is looked after in foster care (Held 2005). Piat (2005) quoted numbers from Montreal (Canada): no less than 1979 psychiatric patients reside in foster homes. In the UK most local authorities organize adult placement. In 8% of the cases, it concerns people with mental health problems* (Van de Walle 2005: 34).

Psychiatric foster care programmes have a lot to offer. Some are more traditional, others are very innovative. Exchanging information and know-how is highly recommended at this stage but it is not enough. It is clear that more research is needed as to the clinical effects of psychiatric fostering. In this area, Geel may play an important role. If there is solid evidence that a client's condition and perceived quality of life significantly improve, it might be easier to get the system recognized and adopted as an essential and valuable component within the range of community care services offered to people with enduring and severe psychiatric illnesses.

| Chapter III |
The organization as it is today[7]

The larger framework

In 1983 a Regional Psychiatric Clinic, called "Sanokliniek" (the Sano Clinic), was established to meet the needs of patients with psychiatric problems in the area. From the very start, the clinic formed a partnership with the traditional psychiatric foster care programme, an uncomfortable partnership, indeed. It certainly took some time for people to get used to the idea that a world-famous, centuries-old, entirely open family care system was twinned with a socially closed, classic mental hospital. At first glance, the two divisions seemed strange bedfellows, and in many ways they were. The management in those days strictly separated the two and did anything but encourage transfer of know-how and look for synergy. Following a change of management in the late nineties, though, the two divisions did start to look for common ground and the organization got consolidated. However, even today the scars as a result of a totally different approach of the two divisions by the management are still visible.

In 1991 the Psychiatric Foster Care Programme and the Regional Psychiatric Clinic were officially incorporated in the State Psychiatric Hospital Geel (*Openbaar Psychiatrisch Ziekenhuis Geel*, abbreviated OPZ Geel or OPZ). At the same time the organization was transferred from the Federal to the Flemish Government and psychiatric foster care in Geel was officially recognized by Royal Decree. According to the official definition, psychiatric foster care is a form of hospitalization for patients whose psychological and social equilibrium can only be attained and preserved by means of permanent care. In this particular case the care is provided by a foster family under the therapeutic supervision of a multidisciplinary team that operates within the framework of a psychiatric hospital.

In April 2006 the name changed yet again; henceforth it is called *"Openbaar Psychiatrisch Zorgcentrum Geel"* ("State Psychiatric Care Centre Geel"). The term "Hospital" has been removed from the name, as mental health care's main focus is increasingly on community care and the total range of services offered by the organization. A stay in hospital tends to be fairly short and is seen as a temporary arrangement.

Comparing our research notes of the 1970s and 2000, we observe striking and telling differences in the terminology used. This is symbolic for the chosen path towards a more "professional" approach. In 2000, staff members, foster parents and patients were expected to have replaced the term *"kolonie"* ("colony") with "OPZ" or *"gezinsverpleging"* ("foster family care"). *"Kostgever"* (lit. "board giver") should have been replaced by *"pleeggezin"* ("foster

7 This chapter mainly draws on non-published OPZ materials.

family"), *"pleegmoeder"* ("foster mother") or *"pleegvader"* ("foster father"). *"Kostgast"* ("male boarder") and *"kostmens"* ("female boarder") supposedly made way for *"patiënt/e"* ("patient"), and *"sectiewachter"* ("section guard" or "supervisor") for *"wijkverpleegkundige"* ("district nurse"), a term with a more professional ring to it. The district nurses were consistently resorting to this new terminology when talking to patients and families, trying their best to make these new labels stick. Without much success, however, as families continued to use the traditional terminology. *"Kostgevers"* generally could not perceive their traditional system as a sort of extended psychiatric hospital. These days the term *"cliënt"* ("client") is being introduced in official documents to point out that people are not thought of as being "ill" or "dependent on care" as the word "patient" seems to imply. This sort of nuance is completely lost on some members of staff, let alone on the foster families.

In the wake of the introduction of new terminology, other measures were taken by the management team to professionalize the organization as a whole and the foster care programme specifically. In 2000, a five-year strategic plan for the OPZ was developed. One of its most important aspects was a complete reorganization of all services into four quasi-autonomous divisions, each one focusing on a specific target group: adults, elderly, youngsters and rehabilitation. Each one of these divisions is run by a manager and a psychiatrist. All teams provide comprehensive care and are thus multidisciplinary. There are nurses, social workers, psychiatrists, psychologists, and occupational therapists. The general idea was to create smaller entities which would be far more flexible, agile and more in touch with the needs of their target group. This reorganization went hand in hand with a significant investment in infrastructure, professional staff, training and new services. Currently the OPZ offers a wide array of psychiatric services ranging from community care to in-patient treatment programmes. The number of people reached and supported has doubled in five years time. The organization has changed beyond recognition, but, then again, it hasn't. Even though it has expanded, it has retained its warm and human approach and its close ties with the surrounding community. Even though new services have been developed, the foster family care programme is still at its core, its main source of inspiration and to some extent its conscience as well. As Raj Persaud aptly put it in his radio series Travels of the Mind (BBC 2003):

> *"Geel is a small town which acts like one big hospital. This really is care in the community. Today, Geel has world class psychiatric facilities but is virtually unique as a place where mentally ill inhabitants lead normal, useful lives in the homes of local residents."*

Psychiatric foster care is the single biggest component of the rehabilitation division. This division, started up in its present form in 2004, provides balanced care for people with long-term mental disorders. The main aims are to minimize long-term disability from mental illness and to protect personal dignity. Apart from the foster care programme, the division groups several residential facilities (90 beds in total), workshops, community centres, an admission programme, two day-activity centres and a leisure service. All professionals focus on helping clients map out their wishes and expectations and establish what the latter can do on their own and where they need assistance. The professionals and the foster parents associated with the OPZ both accept the clients—as far as possible—the way they are. The general idea is to improve the client's quality of life and thus facilitate recovery. A strategy paper was published mid-2006 in which the future of the division is being discussed. It implies quite a few changes, some of which will also affect the foster care programme. As stated in the previous chapter, foster parents will play an active part in the policymaking process.

Organization of foster care

The psychiatric foster care programme recruits foster families in both Geel and its neighbouring towns. To organize family care, the territory is divided in twelve districts. Each district groups 25 to 35 families which are visited by the same district nurse. The district nurses function as clinical case managers. When they are on leave, they are replaced by a member of the team. As it stands today, a team groups three district nurses, a social worker and a GP. Towards the end of 2006, once the new guidelines will have been implemented, a team will consist of a coordinator, a part-time psychiatrist, a part-time GP, four district nurses, a social worker, and an occupational therapist. A psychologist is available on demand. Currently, there are four teams. By the end of 2006 there will be three. The idea is that each multidisciplinary team will be housed in a centre in town: one catering to the north of Geel, one to the west and one to the south. In these centres patients and their foster families will be able to talk to members of the team, consult a GP, a psychiatrist or psychologist. Apart from the professional contact, patients can come to the centre to work or relax and take part in activities. The main advantages of decentralizing the professional care are that the link with the Hospital will be less obvious and the teams will be more closely involved with what is going on in the district. It should also be easier to bridge the perceived gap between the professionals and the foster families. A centre in town is easier to access and not as distant and formal as a psychiatric hospital; the threshold to come and talk to people should certainly be lower.

Clinical case management

The district nurses regularly pop in on the family—at the very least once a month—to ensure that everything is going smoothly and to deliver the prescribed medication. In case problems arise, the frequency of the visits substantially increases. Families are entitled to help around the clock. The nurses act as contacts, confidents and advocates for patient and family. They monitor the interaction between the patient and the foster family. In case of problems they mediate, report on the patient's behaviour or intervene if necessary. If problems are too serious for the nurse and family to cope with on their own, the nurse can report the problem at either his/her team meeting, or s/he can present it at the weekly staff meeting chaired by the medical director. In that sense the Geel system is more professionally advanced than often thought to be the case. Folk tradition and present-day psychiatry do go hand in hand.

Foster families are entitled to having their patients readmitted any time. Legally speaking, it is their right. From an ethical point of view, though, it is a different matter, for one cannot allow patients to be subject to arbitrary treatment. The OPZ and foster parents have a silent agreement that patients cannot be turned away without a good reason. The reverse also holds of course. If a foster parent commits serious abuse, the district nurse may recommend the patient's instant readmission to hospital. "Pulling out" the patient is seen as a major blame

District nurse is key-figure of professional system
(Photo K. Herzog)

and is a measure that is only taken in cases of serious neglect or harassment. One of the nurses who once took such action told us she was threatened by the foster family that had thus fallen into disrepute.

The district nurse is not only a counsellor but also a nurse in the strict sense of the word. If the patient falls ill, the nurse is the first to be contacted. The nurse can decide that hospitalization and further medical treatment is necessary, or that the team physician is consulted at once. The nurse is also the one who accompanies the patient to the general hospital or to other medical facilities for consultation, surgery or other major treatments. Sometimes this takes up quite a lot of time.

On a day-to-day basis the nurse is the key-figure of the "professional" system. Psychologists, physicians and psychiatrists rarely visit the homes and only get in touch with the foster families when major problems arise. Foster parents who do not agree with a nurse's decision or attitude can contact the programme manager or the ombudswoman. In the near future they will also be able to contact the coordinator of the centre in their district, or make an appointment with the psychiatrist and/or psychologist. Feeling the need of lots of foster families and patients, the current psychiatrist has made a point of planning more home visits, so that he doesn't only see families and patients when they are in distress. Prevention and stabilization are the keywords here.

According to the foster parents, the relationship between the members of the nursing team and the foster families is generally excellent. Our own observations confirm this. During the interviews older foster parents sometimes reminisced about the past. Whenever they compared the former "section guards" with the present staff, the latter invariably came out on top.

In-patient care

As is stated in the WHO document on Balanced Care (2003), one cannot provide balanced care without some psychiatric in-patient care. The history of Geel (cf. *Chapter I*) attests to that. The unit in the OPZ (30 beds) plays a crucial role. It is primarily used for patients who urgently need medical assessment, who suffer from severe psychiatric relapses and behavioural disturbances, or from acute neuropsychiatric conditions. Sometimes the unit merely offers a time-out, both for the foster parents and the client. Even a short stay might help clear up a messy situation. The unit is also used as "hotel" to offer temporary relief to families while they are travelling. Last but not least, the unit hosts both clients who are looking for a new foster home and new clients who are attending the mandatory observation programme. Those patients who suffer from old age and severe concomitant physical disorders are referred to a unit in the Division for the Elderly (20 beds).

Admission procedure

If a mental health worker, legal guardian or family member fills out an admission form, the application is first assessed by the medical director and then presented to the admission board. The admission criteria are mostly of a functional nature and assess the patients' ability to live together with other people. Patients suitable for family care typically have chronic psychiatric problems such as schizophrenia, personality and mood disorders, etc. (cf. *Introduction*). Importantly, their condition is stabilized, aggression is under control and there is no history of sexual offences or crime. A significant group of patients combines mental retardation with psychiatric disorders. Patients should be capable of emotional attachment, some form of communication, and doing things independently. If an applicant is bedridden or too dependent, this is seen as a negative point. Patients who are quite advanced in age and/or infirm do not stand a good chance of being admitted. Whatever the pathology is, it must be fairly stabilized. Important is that applicants are able to cope with daily life, bond with family members, accept authority, and tune in to the family's life and patterns of expectation.

Clearly not everyone is eligible. A recent study by Wilfried Bogaerts, an OPZ psychologist, makes clear which types of recent cases have been successfully integrated in the Geel foster family system. For the sake of illustration, we selected ten of the twenty-eight cases described in the study (Bogaerts 1999):

> **Case 1:** mild mental handicap, 38 years old, male, paranoid schizophrenia, almost entirely socially isolated (no longer tolerated by his own family), no anchoring.
>
> **Case 2:** mild mental handicap, 21 years old, male, living at the edge of society (hopeless situation), neglected, aggression due to lack of structure in the family situation.
>
> **Case 3:** mild mental handicap, 62 years old, female, self-neglect after spouse's demise, unable to look after herself.
>
> **Case 4:** mild mental handicap, 40 years old, male, married twice, depression combined with obsessions leading to hospitalization in a psychiatric clinic, few social contacts.
>
> **Case 5:** mild mental handicap, 35 years old, female, was married, social problems and flight, hyper-sexuality, psychiatric decompensation after marital problems.
>
> **Case 6:** mild mental handicap, 47 years old, male, epilepsy, hallucinations, was living with parents at the time of his admission to a psychiatric clinic.
>
> **Case 7:** normally gifted, 56 years old, female, divorced, five children, psychotic decompensation with schizoid personality (destroyed her house in psychotic outburst), isolated after divorce, shaky motivation with respect to foster family care.

Case 8: low IQ and mild mental handicap, 48 years old, female, divorced, four children, self-neglect and passive attitude, didn't manage in sheltered accommodation followed by hospitalization in psychiatric clinic, applied for foster family care due to lack of alternatives.

Case 9: normally gifted although at low end, 27 years old, male, schizophrenic, lack of initiative, sectioned for reasons of confusion and aggression.

Case 10: normally gifted, 46 years old, male, schizophrenic, was living with his mother. When in general hospital, the patient was referred to a psychiatric clinic for reasons of regression.

Most of the remaining eighteen patients also decompensated after the family structure had collapsed or the key figure in their life had disappeared. Patients who used to live in a family structure in which others took the lead are generally well-suited for the Geel system. Integration comes naturally as foster care merely continues the support once provided by the relative(s). According to the author, foster care is particularly tailored to the needs of this type of patients.

Matching

Finding the right family for the right patient is no easy feat. Indeed, both parties need to be properly matched. When patients first come to Geel, they are formally admitted to the hospital. During the day they attend a programme in the Observation House, an ordinary house in the street. There is a maximum of eight patients living together with two coaches. Most stay there for about three months. Patients have domestic duties (cooking, ironing, gardening, etc.), work on their general skills and find out what it means to live together. They go shopping, go out for a drink, pick up books at the library, get acquainted with public transport, etc. Some also get a refresher course in traffic regulations; others learn to ride their bicycle in heavy traffic. They assume responsibilities and share. In the meanwhile the coaches find out what the patients' wishes, desires and expectations are, and they monitor and assess their behaviour when confronted with stressful situations. They also map out their clients' strengths. Importantly, the patient gets the time to slowly grow used to the idea that henceforth s/he is going to live in a family context and to start thinking about the sort of family that might suit him/her. Would s/he prefer a young family, possibly with children, or a more mature family, a single parent set-up or a couple? A family in the centre of town or in the country? How do they feel about pets? The coaches regularly report to the admission team headed by the medical director-psychiatrist. Building on this information, the admission team decides if the patient is suitable for family care and, if so, what sort of family is a good match. If all goes well, the liaison officer will contact the district nurses and together they will start scouting for a suitable family. Having simultaneously considered the wishes of the candidate-foster families, the liaison officer usually comes up with a few suggestions. A young family with four daughters, e.g., may have a preference for a female patient, while a foster family with two grown-up sons might prefer a male. Over the years, the district nurses have gathered an impressive amount of information about the potential candidate-families. Once both the patient and the family give a green light, the patient moves in. The district nurse monitors the integration of the patient in the host family.

As for foster parents, there is no clear-cut profile. There are single-parent families, widows and widowers, retired people, young families, farmers, blue- or white-collar workers, poor people, wealthy people, etc. Important is that the homes are caring, stable and able to cope with stressful situations. Moreover, a regular income is required and sufficient space to lodge one or more guests. Of course, the children need to agree and people need to be fully aware of what it means to live with a psychiatric patient. Families do not receive training about psychiatric illnesses. The secret of the success of family care lies in the ordinary, “non-therapeutisised”, “common sense” approach. Finally, the candidate-foster parent must be in good health and cannot suffer from any contagious diseases like tuberculosis or hepatitis B. (This rule goes back to the times when a lot of tuberculosis was around.) Moreover, his/her profession must be compatible with the responsibilities as a foster parent. Bartenders, e.g., are excluded. As a rule, the foster parent must live in Geel or in one of the neighbouring villages. Foster parents are not allowed to take in persons who are under the supervision of other institutions. A Geelian family is entitled to host up to three patients in their home. There used to be a rule specifying patients in one household needed to be of the same gender. This rule was abandoned years ago. Gender is no longer an issue as long as the patients are compatible and get along fine. Requirements regarding the quality of the home and the patients’ rooms are meticulously laid down by the law.

| Chapter IV |
Case studies

The 19 case studies or sketches below are carefully selected out of a series of 108. They are based on fieldwork conducted in two stages, 1999-2000 and 2005-2006. The passages which refer to the second stage of the research are discussed separately and are marked as such. The data collected during the interviews have been amply discussed and verified with the district nurses in charge of the respective families and their guests.

In these methodological-qualitative case studies we aim at characterising the Geel foster family care system as accurately and lively as possible. Our vantage point is invariably the narrative and observations of both the foster families and their guests. After the descriptive stage we confront the data with current rehabilitation theory. We try to establish to what extent the foster family care system meets the criteria of good community care.

The cases presented below show a partial overlap: what goes for case 1 may also hold for case 2. For instance, both families have in common that relationships within the family are very cordial and warm. However, one needs to be aware that families have been added to the selection because they bring new aspects of the family care system to light. Basically, the aim is to present as complete a picture of foster family care as possible. Ultimately, this series of cases represents the diversity of the Geel system, and highlights its inordinate capacity to offer tailor-made solutions and cater to patients' personal and individual needs. The organizing principle in the case studies below is an ever-increasing level of difficulty to live under one roof. The first few cases are showcases of harmonious and peaceful relationships between hosts and guests, be it that the contexts significantly vary. As one reads on, though, one gets confronted with more taxing relationships and inevitable crises. The last three cases (17-19) deal with different situations: one family was completely new to the system, and two other families live in the periphery of Geel. All names are pseudonyms.

1) A 'son' and a 'guest'

2000

An old house with a garden in one of the hamlets in Geel. Both foster parents are well into their 70s. A married daughter, who currently lives in another town, is visiting. Pros (73) is also present. Fons (62), the other guest, walks in at the end of the session. The atmosphere is happy and relaxed, people laugh a lot. When the foster father, Louis, complains that his wife, Trien, does not leave him much room in bed, Pros jokes that he is not too old to get a divorce. The foster mother has just returned from hospital where she had surgery, and the family is anxiously expecting a message about the health of one of the grandchildren who got concussed.

Louis used to be a factory worker while his wife managed a small farm, a classic formula at the time. There are four daughters in the family, all of them married, and numerous grandchildren and great-grandchildren. The daughter present in the discussion stresses that she and her sisters were as good as raised by "guests". The youngest daughter is 33 at the time of the interview. Pros has always played with the children and he still does so when the grandchildren visit. He is a very happy, radiant sort of fellow, who is very sociable and enjoys company. His behaviour is very normal, indeed.

All present are very positive about the Geel foster care system. The daughter points out, however, and everybody agrees, that, in former days, quite a number of guests were exploited by "large farmers". Now things have considerably improved. In the distant past, "the sick" sometimes lived in the barn and ate whatever they were served. The daughter: "Many farmers made their fortune exploiting these lads! They were only interested in the 'good', read 'strong' patients." Pros confirms that they worked him hard at his former "post".

Pros offers that he is ever so pleased with his present home. He arrived here some thirty years ago. Back then, he had asked Louis, whom he had occasionally encountered in the fields while still working with his former foster father, if he could come and live at his home.

The foster parents are pretty sure that Pros would have never been sent to Geel nor to any other mental institution had someone taken care of him earlier on in life. Pros is an orphan and came to Geel after World War II. After two years, he was set free and had a job tending gardens. But Pros could not cope and suffered from severe palpitations. At the time of the Brussels World Expo, in 1958, Pros had an African girlfriend for quite a while. Pros also helped DJs in dance-halls. He used to practise various sports, mostly jogging. Pros is also a fisherman at the OPZ club. His parents reckon his behaviour is entirely normal. Pros' memory and conversation are perfect. He spends his annual holiday in Spain. Every week he cleans the house of one of the daughters. He has always been very helpful and expedient. All the children and grandchildren are fond of him. Pros is "babysitter-in-chief". About his relations with children he states: "I do not even need to say anything, I can just do it, I guess!" One of the granddaughters is writing a dissertation on Pros' life. In the course of our conversation the 11-year-old grandson phones from the hospital that he is doing fine, and that they must give his best to Pros. Pros wishes him well and tells him to come home soon. To sum up: in this family the social relations are friendly and warm.

Fons, the other patient arrived in the family merely six years ago. He was sent to Geel when he was sixteen. During the day he works at the OPZ. He isn't home yet. His foster parents and the others present do not perceive him as an easy guy. He is terribly egocentric, overeats all the time, flatters his foster mother, and fakes pain in order to dodge errands and other minor assignments. Fons makes mistakes on purpose just to get dismissed from the job. Pros has no time for that kind of behaviour. Fons takes plenty of medication, yet remains very nervous.

Fons visits his natural family three days a year. Every week he pays a visit to a nearby supermarket that gives away small presents on Saturdays. He loves cakes. Fons is a soccer fan, and knows exactly what goes on in this area: which club sold or bought whom, etc.

When Fons enters the room, everybody is strikingly kind to him. He tells us that he works as a gardener at the OPZ and is in charge of weeding. He crosses Geel by bike in all possible directions but always starts from the centre, lest he gets disoriented. Learning how to make shortcuts is too much to ask.

All people present confirm the immense success of a popular Flemish singer, Jules Kabas. This comedian used to perform for the patients at the OPZ. His by now traditional question to the audience went: "What do you want me to sing?" The audience would always shout back: "Only the loonies work!" (the title of one of his songs "*'t Zijn zotten die werken!*"). Success was guaranteed. The patients absolutely enjoyed listening to this song: a sure sign of black humour.

The family wonders what will happen to the Geel system. The daughter says that she would take in a patient, if only she lived in Geel. One thing is for sure: as soon as the parents are no longer able to care for him, Pros can go and live with one of the other daughters.

In their long career, the foster parents have given a home to eight other patients. One of them was French, César. César was quite a character. The foster mother was able to control him, but it demanded considerable stamina. Whenever he came home infuriated, by the back door, she took her children to their uncle's place by the front door. Only then did she confront César.

When we leave, all present invite us to revisit as there has been no time to talk things through thoroughly. We kindly accepted the invitation and returned a few weeks later.

2006

Six years ago, shortly after our first visit in 1999, the foster mother died. The foster father (88) underwent serious surgery two years ago. That's why he can no longer cope on his own. Pros (80) recently suffered from a cerebral haemorrhage but has recovered well over the past two months; he can walk again and has attended the local fishing competition. He is very optimistic about his recovery and is friendly and jovial as ever. The other patient, Fons, has moved to another family; but then, things were never that great with Fons.

The youngest daughter of the family lives nearby and has taken on the care for the two elderly men. They now live downstairs. They sleep in the former living-room which has been transformed into a bedroom. Before she leaves for work, the daughter drops in and prepares breakfast. Later, a help takes over until the daughter comes back late afternoon. In the evening, a nurse comes in to check up on the men and help them in bed. At night the men look after one another.

Originally, the OPZ had decided to transfer Pros to a retirement home, but both the foster father and Pros heavily protested; they won the argument. The daughter admits it would have felt all wrong to "abandon" Pros in a home. She emphasizes that he has become one of them, and that the grandchildren and Pros are like two peas in a pod, just like in the old days. So the original plan that Pros would go and live with one of the daughters was carried out. The daughter started working part-time to be able to look after him properly.

Comment[8]

This case exemplifies the ideal type of relationship within a foster family according to most insiders, foster families included: mother and father have been married for ever; they have scores of children, grandchildren and even great-grandchildren. They all live in a network of warm family relations. One takes adversity as far as personal health is concerned in one's stride. Humour is a crucial ingredient in one's daily life. The guests are an integral part of this substantial family group. Pros is more integrated than Fons. Pros has been accepted by the family as he is, without reserve. They all love him and do not think of him as abnormal. Pros, an orphan, cannot cope in the wider community on his own and needs support. That is his "shortcoming". As already mentioned, research by Bogaerts (1999), demonstrates that clients who lack or have suddenly lost a family figure who guides and supports them, are particularly well-suited for the Geel foster care system. Pros endears himself to the family because of his excellent relationship with the children and grandchildren. He also makes himself useful by lending a helping hand in horticulture, by cleaning the daughter's house and by doing some odd jobs around the house. It makes him feel good about himself. The value of his work is socially recognized. In addition, Pros plays sports. In doing so, he is in contact with broader social circles, outside the family.

Fons has also been accepted by the family but keeps more distance than Pros. Obviously, everybody is well aware of his shortcomings, Pros included. Some of his quaint characteristics are rather disapproved of because they are seen as signs of disingenuous behaviour. Fons flatters, manipulates and will act up to avoid chores. The upside is that Fons holds a job and manages to establish contact with the Geel community in his spare time through his love of sports. Fons is obviously less likeable than Pros, but that doesn't mean he is rejected. The foster family and the wider family accept him with the shortcomings that cannot be overcome.

The family recognizes that the psychiatric foster care system hasn't always been a bed of roses: in the past, a few farmers prospered thanks to the cheap labour of patients in their care. That time is not all that distant, as people like Pros still remember it. Again and again the fact that there used to be abuse surfaces in conversations. Mostly one alludes to the past, but occasionally that is not the case: every so often a foster parent refers to a current situation. César's story clearly demonstrates that conflicts with some guests are inevitable and are part and parcel of the system. Our interviewees do not tend to idealize the Geel system. One of the family's daughters intends to "adopt" Pros when the parents can no longer cope.

In the above analysis most important characteristics of rehabilitation, as outlined in recent studies, are distinctly present. Comparing the facts in this particular case with the guidelines by Bachrach (Bachrach 1990: 37-42), one can conclude Geel foster family care easily qualifies as "best practice":

1. Guests are approached as individuals.
2. The social environment of the foster family adjusts itself to the guests' needs.

8 In the following case studies we only add a comment if we want to highlight certain facts or implications that haven't emerged in the interviews. For a synthesis based on all 108 cases we refer to *Chapter V*.

3. Care givers build on the guests' remaining strengths.
4. The atmosphere is generally positive and optimistic, there is humour and laughter.
5. Guests perform chores according to their abilities and feel useful as a result.
6. Guests fill in their spare time as they wish. This results in contacts outside the family circle.
7. The patients' lifestyle and the choices they make in life develop in a spontaneous, dialectic relationship between the family members, outside the walls of an institution.
8. Continuity of care is virtually a hallmark of the Geel system. More often than not the care is passed on from one generation to the next.

Together with the district nurse and the OPZ team, the members of both the foster family and wider family circle form a full-fledged case management team. The only difference is that they do not merely follow up on the client at regular intervals. Instead, they live together with the client, day after day, all year round. If necessary, a psychiatrist can be consulted. As opposed to some "disenfranchised movements" that lay a firm claim on the label "rehabilitation" (Bachrach 1995), Geel does not show any disdain for the medical profession and psychiatry in particular. Actually, it embraces scientific advances. We have spoken to more than one family who is an advocate of more structural contact with a psychiatrist.

The care given in the above case is in line with Bennett's description of psychiatric rehabilitation: "The process that helps a person with limited possibilities to make optimal use of his remaining capabilities, so as to function in as normal a social context as possible." (quote in Pieters & Peuskens 1995: 13)

2) Two senior sons and "a mighty irritable fellow"

2000

A splendid, brand-new mansion with an impressive, three-hectare garden, a pond, stables and a summer house with a guestroom, located close to the family business. The foster mother, Lisa, is in her early forties, in sharp contrast with her guests, Fabien (80), Florent (78) and Albert (65). Age differences notwithstanding, Albert refers to Lisa as "mum". He repeats time and again that he loves his mum to bits.

Fabien and Florent have a long history in the family. They used to live with their present foster father's parents. Albert joined the family as recently as 1987. He has been in Geel for more than fifty years, though.

In her own opinion, Lisa has always been socially aware, and that was her motivation to become a foster mother. This explanation looks very plausible. Putting money aside for a rainy day does not seem much of a concern to this very active and successful business woman. One of her daughters, a college graduate who participated in our discussions, plans to take in patients herself once she is established.

It is worthwhile to point out that the family has been through some rough times with some of their former guests. Two young patients caused them quite a lot of grief. At some point one of them injured Lisa with a knife, while the other harassed one of the daughters and repeatedly got involved in fights. Both patients were eventually sent back to the OPZ. These sorts of unfortunate occurrences are not branded as failures in the Geel system. If patients do not settle in a family, they are given a second, or even a third chance in another setting. Of course, this also applies for the foster families. They are quite welcome to try and host another client.

As it is, we are sitting at a generous table in a modern, spacious kitchen. Florent (78) feels a bit poorly during our first visit. A month later though, on our second visit, he is in good health. As we walk in, he is just about to run some errands on his bicycle. Lisa has prepared a note with the items he is to pick up. He is ever so proud to make his own contribution to the household, he says time and again. Florent was born in a very poor family. They lived in a hut in the countryside. He had four sisters. His father caught birds which he sold at the market in Brussels every week. This is what he did to sustain his family. Every week, Florent and his father travelled to Brussels by bicycle, carrying their load. Florent is still quite knowledgeable about birds, but complains that bird-catching is no longer possible “as nets aren’t available”. He recites a long list of birds. At some point Florent was no longer able to support himself. Relatives suggested to Lisa there had been episodes of violence in the family; there was even talk of shots having been fired. Fact is that Florent broke down; the exact details about his past are missing.

Forty years on, however, Florent expressed the desire to return to his native village. One day, Lisa fulfilled his wish and drove him there in her convertible. She told us how Florent’s memories came back, bit by bit. He was like a voice-over in a silent movie. He guided Lisa to the place where their hut had once been located. When Lisa and Florent knocked at the door of a relative, the lady banged the door in their face, shouting that there was no inheritance to be had. To see Florent after all these years in the company of an elegant young lady driving a flashy sports car must have been quite a shock.

Albert, in contrast, is a city boy. His father got married twice and Albert witnessed a lot of brawls. Albert currently helps out in the family business. He is very dedicated. He carefully notes down what materials in which quantities various clients take home. Lisa stresses that Albert is perfectly reliable even on busy days when lots of customers come by. Albert is very good at counting.

Albert closely follows the soccer league on TV. When he was younger, he was a keen fisherman. He regularly calls at the house of the mayor of a neighbouring village where he is an honorary guest in family celebrations. Lisa, from her side, organized a huge party for Albert’s 50-year anniversary in Geel. The OPZ social worker managed to release a significant sum, which the foster parents generously doubled. Albert is well and truly honest. When he found 50,000 BEF (approx. $1,660) on the street sometime ago, he brought the sum to the police station straight away. In the course of the three visits we paid his family, Albert interrupted the discussion again and again, eliciting from his foster mother that he was a nice lad and stating: “I love mama very much!”

Splendid house: home to Florent, Fabien and Albert
(Photo E. Roosens)

Albert doesn't identify with the guys who weekly visit the patients' club. He is one of the few men who is allowed to go from door to door on New Year's Eve to wish people well and collect treats. Actually, he is quite entrepreneurial: he sets out twice, on New Year's Eve and merely six days later, on Epiphany. He is the proud owner of a TV-set, a huge collection of glasses, films, about 1,000 records, and more than 2,000 CDs. He also owns four radios. He absolutely loves music and always carries a radio around wherever he goes. "I truly have all I want," he says. Albert arrived in Geel as a young boy, more than 50 years ago. His former foster parents hosted him the first 21 years. Afterwards, he was taken in by another family, where he cooked and helped his foster mother who was bed-ridden. Her death came as a frightful shock to him. Albert went through a terrible time, but eventually he got used to his new home. As for his natural family, Albert has a brother who lives in a mental institution. Another brother got killed in a car accident. His father, a brother and a sister visited him only once in 50 years. His father is dead now.

Fabien usually accompanies one of the company's truck drivers, so he is out a good part of the day. Fabien has an uncontrollable urge to "collect" money and alcoholic beverages. As a result, Lisa has to keep her stock of wine and beer behind locked doors, carefully hiding her keys. Fabien does not know the value of coins and bills, and is not able to read the clock, but "feels" what time it is. "Gitje will be home soon!", he says, when one of the daughters is about to return. Fabien and Lotje, the other daughter, are real pals. Lotje will always protect Fabien when something goes wrong: "He is family." Every so often, Albert has to go and fetch Fabien in a pub when he is "on a bender".

Fabien tends to order his mates about. The minute he wakes up in the morning, everybody is to get out of bed that very instant. "He is an irritable fellow, that's what he is," says his mother, "a chief!" He has his fits and can get quite angry, not mincing his words. One day, he beat Albert with a slipper. "I didn't breathe a word," commented Albert, the wiser one of the two, "I did not react." Fabien is also less obedient towards the foster mother. The way he addresses her is quite informative of his mood. He sometimes calls her "Lisa", other times he calls her "mother", and sometimes even "madam".

Lisa insists that she thoroughly enjoys her guests' company. "Their love comes right from the heart," she says, "it is never fake; they wouldn't know how to be insincere." They care about her too, so much is obvious. When she is ill, they come to her room to find out how she is doing. Lisa has been familiar with foster care from her early childhood onwards. One of her grandmothers used to host guests. Her own mother was socially aware as well, but her job was incompatible with fostering. Lisa admits that "she wouldn't know what to do without the guys." Even though it requires sacrifices and care, "just like for your own children". The three men always accompany the family when they go to parties.

2005

On revisiting this family in November 2005, we roughly found the same well-functioning unit. They had been through rough times, though, suffering from some physical setbacks. Remarkably, the foster parents, their daughters and adopted sons had all bravely faced down their misfortune. If anything, it had strengthened their bond. One of the girls who is now established on her own proved to be a rock and took care of "the men" as best she could.

Florent, now an octogenarian, often has difficulties breathing. He spent some time in hospital. He has recovered now. Being really ill, he had offered his bike, his pride and joy, to his mum as a sort of heirloom with the words: "It is yours now." Presently he is using his bike again; weather permitting, as often as three times a day. He still goes shopping by bike. When the weather is bad, he appeals to one of the girls to take him shopping by car. Occasionally, he lets his mates get the better of him. They persuade him to smuggle in beer for Fabien, still an alcoholic. Strangely enough the money is secretly handed over by Albert, even though he has been Fabien's self-declared victim for a long time. Almost every morning at breakfast there is a bout of aggression. As was the case five years earlier, it is Albert who pacifies the situation. The week before our visit Fabien had been drinking heavily.

A while ago, the truck driver, whom Fabien used to accompany, retired. Fabien still goes on his rounds in the truck provided his personal guardian angel, one of the daughters, drives it. But he has increasingly less things to do. Albert's tasks too have dwindled for technical reasons. He would like to take on more. Florent still does the shopping he can handle. Occasionally, he excels himself. Around All Saints' Day he braved foul weather and walked to the flower shop to buy flowers to honour the grave of his previous foster parents. It is a tradition for Florent, one that he won't give up if he can help it.

Five years onwards, Albert is still the insatiable, incorrigible collector of CDs, videos, records, glasses (spectacles), radios, etc. During our most recent visit we asked permission to go and photograph his collection. Reluctantly, he took us to his room. We praised ourselves lucky we were allowed to photograph his room and video collection. A big cupboard, however, where Albert has been hoarding God knows what forever, remained sealed. His foster mother had warned us that that might happen, since absolutely nobody is allowed anywhere near this cupboard, let alone have a little peek. His secret is respected by the entire family. Albert told me in passing that he still enjoys his soccer.

Towards the end of our visit, the conversation drifted towards the subject of the financial compensation foster parents receive for looking after their guests. The family's opinion on this matter was crystal clear: the amount transferred by the OPZ does not cover expenses. The truth of the matter is that the guests here enjoy a comfortable lifestyle, just like the other members of the family. "Only the best is good enough for us, and that includes them. So we are far from making a profit," Lisa smiled. "We do it because that is who we are. We wouldn't feel whole without them. It is quite simple, really." Lisa adds that she will remain committed even as she is getting on and her health declines. As long as she can handle it, that is. We have no reason whatsoever to doubt her words.

Lisa thinks that the foster care system will survive. She is quick to add, though, that lots of young people will opt out. Taking in patients means too many sacrifices, like staying at home "and if there is one thing these modern madams thoroughly dislike, then it is exactly that." Another problem is the financial aspect. Foster family care is not exactly a lucrative enterprise. If one is committed to preserve the system for the future, one badly needs to raise the monthly allowance. In 2002 the OPZ as good as pledged it would do so. Unfortunately, as was discussed in *Chapter II*, the federal government wasn't in a hurry to commit more money.

Fabien in front of the family's private fish pond
(Photo E. Roosens)

Comment
This particular case study undoes a common perception that foster families are invariably small farmers who host guests to employ them as farmhands and, in doing so, make a handsome profit. This truly magnificent mansion with its astonishing gardens and comfortable guesthouse offers a very nice and admittedly rather exceptional home to these three men. Actually, it is the exact opposite of how one tends to picture a psychiatric institution.

Remarkably, the three guests, irrespective of their advanced ages and obvious limitations, are all still active. One gets the impression that the men have been influenced by the busy and entrepreneurial atmosphere in the family and ended up completely "adjusted". The fact that they like to work feels authentic and comes across as spontaneous. Work is certainly not "inflicted" on them.

In contrast with the message I got in lots of families, one of the daughters, a college graduate, is determined to host patients herself once she gets established. The way in which Lisa deals with and exercises her authority over "her men", is not based on literature or scholastic knowledge. Nor was the OPZ the source of her wisdom, nor the author of her approach. And yet, everybody is perfectly content and the household runs like clockwork. Life is as spontaneous as it gets with very happy and upbeat moments and adversity as well. The fine thing is that the difficult times only strengthen the bond between the family members. They support one another. This is anything but "artificial" therapy. Actually, it has almost nothing to do with therapy. As a matter of course, this family does not require the OPZ professionals to intervene. The family functions autonomously. Even so, the yearly visit by the Catholic chaplain "who stops by to see how things are" is greatly appreciated.

3) A mother, a daughter and a daughter/sister

2000
The foster mother, Irène (72), lost her husband ten years ago. He used to work in a factory in the vicinity of Geel. Irène used to own a shop but eventually she was forced out due to heavy competition from neighbouring supermarkets. Through her business, Irène got in touch with lots of people. As such she is quite well-known. When we visited the house for the first time, Mireille, the younger patient, was making coffee in the kitchen. The table was laid for coffee and cakes, a daily habit.

Irène is a very enthusiastic lady who, together with her two female guests, tries to make the best of life. Her positive attitude is clearly contagious. The way the three women relate reflects genuine friendship. They call themselves "the three musketeers", meaning that they are always together and share their experiences.

A couple of years ago, when she turned 50, Mireille was thrown a hell of a party. Irène proudly shows me dozens of photographs. The entire family, children included, as well as neighbours of various socio-economic strata joined in. One of the neighbours present was a medical specialist. It was definitely the place to be that day. A party tent was put up in a neighbour's yard. Her friends gave Mireille a beautiful golden necklace and her foster mother gave her a splendid ring. Mireille was happy as a lark with her jewels. Mireille has a fairly low IQ and is unable to actively participate in a conversation. She has to think hard before uttering a sentence. Her short-term memory doesn't work all that well. She is really attached to her foster mother and has a very strong emotional bond with her. In discussions, she constantly and explicitly concurs with her foster mother.

Julia (74), the second patient, is rather aloof and keeps to herself. Before coming to Geel, she spent thirty years in a closed mental institution. Julia has a son and daughter, but is reluctant to talk about them. Her husband left her ages ago.

The three women agree that the Geel system must be continued whatever it takes. It gives hundreds of otherwise unfortunate people a chance to experience happiness in a real home with genuine relationships. The foster mother is convinced that there are enough young people out there who are willing to take on the job of foster parent. The three women have the impression that the system has picked up again the last few years.

In spite of her optimistic nature, Irène is not inclined to idealize the foster care programme. She too was confronted with the downsides of it in her time. After World War II, when she had her shop, she hosted a male patient who, as it turned out, badly deceived her a long time. The man was well-educated, commanded both French and English on top of his native language, and allegedly looked quite normal. While behaving respectfully and friendly, he embezzled quite a lot of Irène's money. She caught on eventually and managed to catch him in the act. She did not send him away, however. The patient disappeared on his own initiative through his bedroom window in the middle of the night. Much later, he was arrested by the police somewhere in France. He happened to be riding a bicycle with a fake tax registration. He confessed that he had stolen money from his foster mother and had run away from Geel. With the stolen money he had bought second-hand bicycle parts which he had hidden in the fields. And then, one day, he had raided his foster mother's shop for food, assembled the bike and fled.

Irène wasn't discouraged by this negative experience; she bounced right back. She stresses that her two present partners are precious to her: they keep her company and she is never lonely. Together they enjoy life. If she was on her own, she probably would not be able to muster the courage to cook, clean, or tend her garden. As it is, the threesome all work together and have fun. The patients carry out odd jobs around the house, while Irène takes care of the rest and does the gardening.

2005

Five years on, in 2005 as I revisit the family, nothing seems to have changed at all. I get a royal welcome with coffee, delicious patisserie and the compliment that they are overjoyed to see me again. Irene announces all is well, and that they are still the three musketeers. Irène proudly produces a medal and certificate she received in honour of her 50th anniversary as foster parent.

Mireille lays the table, cuts the cake and makes coffee, assisted by her "mum" who continuously prompts her what to do next. Mireille's short-term memory hasn't gotten any better over the years, so she has trouble remembering the different steps to successfully complete a task. Her mum does that for her. Mireille is still spoiled rotten. No sooner have we walked in than she shows off a magnificent gold wristwatch, yet another present from her doting foster mother.

Julia is 80 now. Silently she sits at the table until she has eaten her cake. The minute she has finished, she starts clearing away things, even if other people are still savouring their food. Without being flustered, Irène intervenes. She acknowledges that this is a firmly established routine which obviously cannot be broken. When I stop by, a few days later, to drop off some photos, Julia is dusting the furniture, one of her chores. She briefly glances at me and continues dusting without taking any notice of me.

Every year Mireille goes abroad for a week. She relishes her vacation even though she doesn't quite manage to talk about her experiences. Mireille also continues to participate in other activities organized by the OPZ.

At the age of 78, Irène doesn't contemplate abandoning her hobby: as a keen gardener she grows different types of pumpkins, with various shapes, forms and colours. Half a day a week she "gets a hand from a lad" in the neighbourhood. Irène has never travelled. Her home is known as an open house, everybody is welcome. Lots of people stop by for a chat and a cup of coffee. Relations with the neighbours are excellent.

Comment

This case shows integration at its best, people do not hold back at all. The entire kin group and neighbourhood of the foster family attended the 50th-anniversary celebrations of a patient. The love and warmth towards Mireille were real enough. She got gifts from her family and neighbours; she was and is truly one of them. The foster father died 15 years ago. A daughter too died prematurely. Even so, together they overcame these tragedies. As ever, the three musketeers radiate and seem to own the patent on optimism and good cheer. Irène cannot emphasise enough that her companions have saved her from loneliness and motivate her to remain active, day after day. The benefits are mutual: single parents do not get isolated, whereas guests get a home.

4) Brotherhood of men

2000

An older farm at the outskirts of Geel. We first visited this place about 25 years ago, when writing our first book about the Geel system. The patient still remembers that particular visit and so do we. As we walked in that day, in the late morning that was, the three brothers had just returned from the field to have lunch. Wardje, the "guest", had cleaned the house and ordered them to leave their filthy boots outside. We distinctly remember that. They invited us to join them for a meal, and Wardje, who also doubled as a cook, served the soup.

As we revisited in the late nineties, one of the three brothers had died seven years previously. The house and its furniture were still identical. Visitors entered the house through the backdoor. Wardje sat close to the *"Leuvense stoof"* (a well-known traditional coal burner), the best place in the room which Wardje "inherited" from his deceased foster mother. Following her death, he immediately claimed her place and has since refused to cede it to

Wardje firmly in charge of the household
(Photo E. Roosens)

anybody. The reunion with the interviewer was warm and cordial. Wardje repeated again and again that he remembered the first visit.

The family has a long tradition of fostering. Parents and grandparents on both sides of the family, all of farming stock, have hosted patients as long as anybody can remember. They invariably had two men, but Wardje put a stop to that. He could and would not abide competition and always "put his foot down" when there was talk of adopting a second guest. Wardje does the cooking and runs the household the way his late foster mother taught him. When an uncle died last year, Wardje was invited to march in the funeral cortège just behind the dead person's brothers, as a close relative, although the in-laws did not know him and wondered who the hell he was. Wardje belongs to the family under all circumstances, "for better and for worse".

Wardje has always been a keen, almost obsessive, fisherman. Sometimes he was accompanied by one of the brothers, but on most days he went fishing by himself. Then, one day, Wardje got the impression that other members of the OPZ fishing club were poking fun at him. As of that day he refused to go fishing. He stayed home in a huff. His foster fathers could almost feel his frustration and pain and decided to take action. They promptly bought their precious guest a huge private pond (more than a hectare). They then proceeded to put a barbed wire fence around it, so that Wardje could practise his favourite sport undisturbed.

The latter also loves cycling. He is the proud owner of three bikes. The best one is reserved for his Sunday rides. He has got one for work also: Wardje happens to be in charge of all the household shopping and needs a bike to get about. Every day at about 8 p.m., Wardje retires to his room to watch television. He likes watching the news. His favourite programmes, though, are films about flora and fauna. He absolutely adores the documentaries of National Geographic. Wardje never watches the popular commercial station as "they mostly tell lies!" The minute Wardje leaves the room, one of the foster fathers whispers: "He does as he pleases, he is happy here."

At some stage, Wardje bought comfortable bedroom furniture with his own money. He was flabbergasted to learn, a few years later, that the OPZ had decided to replace all patient bedroom furniture with official OPZ hospital beds and closets. Like many other foster families and their guests, Wardje and his foster parents thought this new rule was absurd. Moreover, the goods delivered by the OPZ were low quality compared to the furniture Wardje had purchased. The closet was three times smaller. Still upset, Wardje took us to the room where he had stored his own furniture. "A damn shame," he said, "talk about a waste of money!"

Wardje used to go on vacation to Spain, but his enthusiasm seems to have waned a bit since it involves rising before dawn to catch the plane in Brussels. "Spain and Ibiza are for the young people," he states, "Benidorm, yes, maybe." He would still like to go abroad, but for a few days only. Truth of the matter is, he cannot make up his mind. He may decide to travel to Spain once more, and, then again, he may not. The OPZ urges him to come along, as he is good at keeping difficult room-mates at bay. "If only they gave me a decent room-mate this time," he says almost in despair. "They always promise, but last year they put me up with a guy from Brussels. He went to bed with his socks and shoes on, would you believe it!" Wardje obviously does not think much of "the Colony guys".

The foster parents have the firm hope that one of their nephews will take care of Wardje should they no longer be able to look after him. According to the foster fathers, Wardje used to be "a difficult guy" when he was younger. One had to physically restrain him from time to time, but things gradually improved over the years. Even so, he does have fits from time to time and gets in trouble both with himself and with others, e.g., by changing his mind several times a day about booking his trip to Spain.

When I visited Wardje for the fourth time, he had just been through a stormy week. In spite of assurances, the OPZ had teamed him up with yet another "square" room-mate. Moreover, his pullover which an aunt had knit for him, had been stolen in the hotel, probably by one of the other patients. The foster parents told us behind Wardje's back that tensions had risen very high, indeed, and that their patient had turned violent when contradicted. By the time of our visit he was fairly calm. Years ago Wardje drank a lot, but he no longer does so.

Wardje has a brother who travels around Europe with a circus troupe. Whenever the circus was in the neighbourhood, Wardje's brother used to pop in to say hello. However, the last ten years went by without a sign. To everybody's surprise, at Easter his brother sent him a card with a long poem. Both Wardje and his foster fathers thought this was ridiculous. Sending them a poem, indeed! Wardje has had it with his brother now. "He can go to hell!"

During our second visit in 2000, the atmosphere was even friendlier and the subject of their long years together was discussed at length. The foster fathers couldn't stress enough how important it is to handle patients tactfully and to make them feel included under all circumstances. Wardje shows off his impressive collection of fishing rods and other fishing gear. At my third visit, we had a look at Wardje's immense fishing pond.

Every year the family is visited by a man of Polish descent who spent some time with them after World War II. He was merely a boy then. He had escaped the Germans after his mother had hid him in a toilet. He was initially placed with another foster family in Geel, but, as this family had only daughters, the OPZ transferred him to Wardje's place. After some eighteen months the young man "was set free". He moved to a farm in the town of Diest. He later married but stayed childless. His wife, "a lovely person", always accompanies him on his visits. At every single opportunity he states: "This is the place where I really feel at home!" The foster fathers quote these words with pride and affection.

2005

The minute we enter the home in 2005, a great sadness strikes us. Things have definitely taken a turn for the worse. One of the foster fathers has developed a serious condition and can barely do anything at all. Wardje suffered from brain haemorrhage and is partly paralyzed. He can walk again but with great difficulty. He can forget about cycling. He sold two of his bikes and it cost him dearly. Going to his private pond on fishing expeditions is no longer an option, as he cannot get there. It would be far too strenuous and dangerous to walk along the busy road. Wardje even decided to sell some fishing gear. Housekeeping, washing clothes, are no longer tasks he can perform. Once a week a lady comes in and cleans the house. Food is delivered by meals on wheels. The foster fathers sold their horse a few years ago, which means that they can no longer go on outings with their horse and carriage. Pigs and cows went too. The only remaining "farming" activity is the vegetable patch.

In 2005 we visited the family twice, and each time the inactivity and passive attitude of the threesome grabbed me by the throat. Wardje was sitting next to the stove, as always. The other two men were sitting on a chair in their small sitting room that doubles as dining room. Fortunately, often friends and relatives stop by to chat.

Even though he used to be quite bubbly, Wardje's attitude is far from positive. Three times we heard him say that he would rather have died after his stroke: "I am done with life, I have had it for a long time." We all admonished him that he shouldn't think such thoughts, that he didn't mean what he said; but maybe he did. Wardje was convinced that "they had dragged their feet" in the OPZ Hospital and should have treated him sooner: "They fooled me, they didn't take my complaints seriously." This explains the animosity he seems to have developed towards the OPZ. "The doctor stopped by a few times but now they have forgotten all about me," he alleges and, "had I had a better father," he suddenly reminisces, "I wouldn't have ended up like this. My mum too ended up in an institution in Namur." His foster fathers interrupt this train of thought and tell us that Wardje's father only visited once, as far as they can remember. It was a very long time ago and Wardje, still an adolescent at that time, had run off in a huff. Wardje is quick to add: "He claimed I had been in a madhouse." The psychiatrist had decided he should break all contact with his father. The father was no longer allowed to visit.

Wardje can no longer look after himself. Every week he is picked up by one of the drivers from the Hospital for a bath and a physical. When he falls, he can no longer get up by himself. The only "fit" foster father in the family, a man at the advanced age of seventy-six, needs to pull him up. Not a straightforward task for the latter. Even at night he needs his foster father's assistance to get out of bed when he wants to go to the bathroom. To make things worse, the cable company no longer broadcasts CNN, BBC World and National Geographic, the only programmes Wardje truly enjoyed. And this, as good as immediately after Wardje had purchased a fancy, broad-screen television. To prove his point, Wardje got up and dragged us to his room to admire his now virtually useless TV. Wardje can no longer travel either. At best, he can go with the OPZ to Retie, a neighbouring town. Wardje claims that he is left to his own devises and gets no assistance whatsoever when he has trouble moving about. Wardje "foul-mouthes" his fellow patients: "They no longer work, they sit in the pub all day long! If I were in charge, boy, would things change! Look at me, I worked my whole life!"

But, in spite of all this bad news, the older foster parent strikes a positive note: "You need to take life as it comes, there is no way around it." When Wardje breaks in: "If I were dead, I would be spared all this," he replies: "Yes, that is true, but you wouldn't be around to tell the difference." The foster father whispers to me that he has no idea what will happen to all of them when his mobility goes too. Like the other two, he has recently been in hospital. Fortunately, he was saved in the nick of time. He adds in a loud voice that the neighbours, most of whom are new in the area and live in large and expensive houses, always greet Wardje when they run into him on the street. And then he teases, that all the girls in the neighbourhood wave and smile at Wardje. The latter heavily protests, but is flattered all the same.

The minute Wardje walks out of the room, the old man says: "His head is fine now, but yesterday he was angry as hell. If something is not right, he explodes. It goes up and down." Wardje has made up his mind, he will not be admitted to the OPZ Hospital ever again: "I would rather die!", is the message.

Comment

For a very long time the foster family, three brothers, then two brothers, led a happy and prosperous life with their guest, a key figure in their family. As time went by, the bond between the guys became increasingly close. The foster parents do not complain, not even in these rather hard times. As for Wardje, he doesn't want to leave. He arrived here at the age of 15. The brothers took him in after the death of their parents. This is how this company of men came about. Funnily enough, Wardje automatically took over his foster mother's role in the household, including her seat near the stove which he will not cede under any circumstances. A symbolic act surely. His more senior foster parents have no trouble acknowledging this privilege. The men are all complementary and live celibate lives. A most remarkable family arrangement. Comparing our notes from 2000 with the ones from 2005, it hits us how happy their life together used to be.

After the death of the foster parents, it happens every so often that a single son and a female patient are left behind. In most cases the latter is moved to another family as the care of a female patient by a single male is generally frowned upon. However, occasionally it does happen that the son is left in charge of the female patient, and this brings us to our next case. The man in question has repeatedly told us, that a care situation like his own is quite exceptional. He certainly takes pride in the fact that the authorities placed their trust in him.

5) True siblings*

2000

The foster father, Maurice (71), never married. He took in Zoë (55) following the death of his parents in 1992. Zoë had arrived in the family 28 years ago. Fostering is a long tradition in the family. As long as Maurice can remember, there have always been patients around, both with his parents and grandparents (both sides). Maurice studied up to the age of 19 and then took a job as a factory worker in Liège.

Zoë is a lively and colourful character. She was born in Wallonia. Her native language is French. She attended school to learn Flemish and has basically lost her command of French. As he worked in Liège, her foster father is fluent in both languages. Zoë likes shopping, although adding up gives her a headache. She cannot read either. However, she runs the household perfectly and competently. On weekends she takes off. Saturday afternoons and Sunday are her private time. Every Wednesday afternoon she practises sports and she dances until 8 p.m. When she was younger, Zoë used to drink heavily. She came home tipsy more than once. As she got on, this bad habit sort of petered out. When younger, Zoë also used to

---

* cf. DVD

Entrepreneurial Zoë and her favourite rabbit
(Photo E. Roosens)

"hang out" in cafés with a dubious reputation. No longer so. Now she only visits decent places. At a given time Zoë had a boyfriend, but that relationship ended. According to Zoë, the relationship was doomed anyway.

Zoë talks and talks and talks. Her foster father comments: "She starts talking early in the morning and never stops until she goes to bed." Zoë breeds rare species of rabbits as well as hamsters in a barn and in the garden behind the house. A befriended neighbour sells them for her at the market place. Zoë manages her business without any help. From time to time she is given a lift by a neighbour to pick up leftovers to feed her animals. Zoë cherishes the company of her neighbour's dog, Rex. She pets him several times a day and walks him on weekends. As Zoë works in the garden, the dog sits there and keeps an eye on her. Zoë bought Rex a fancy leash with her own money. Affection is mutual. During our visit Zoë fetched the dog to "introduce" him to us. According to Maurice, Rex is much more concerned about Zoë than about his owner. When a passer-by approaches its home, the dog does not bother to bark. However, when a stranger goes anywhere near Zoë's house, Rex starts barking ferociously. We witnessed this kind of reaction twice. Sadly, Zoë is not allowed to keep a dog of her own, because the foster father reckons their immense garden cannot be fenced off properly.

Zoë is a very active person. She helps Maurice weed the huge garden, she cleans the house and does the cooking. She is not particular about her food and likes everything. In addition, she is a very easygoing person. Maurice would miss her very much if she weren't around. His late parents too, who had taken in their first guest in 1929 and had thus accumulated a lot of experience, enormously appreciated Zoë's contribution to the household.

Zoë is quite popular both in the neighbourhood and in many pubs in Geel. She receives a lot of presents, mostly clothes. These even include quite expensive pieces that well-to-do neighbours have discarded. Zoë owns several fur coats. Nobody would take her for a boarder when she leaves the house, all made up.

Zoë is at the forefront of emancipation too. She is the only female patient who actively participates in the fishing competitions. Her former boyfriend urged her to join the club. "It truly is much more fun when women compete!", he had argued. As it turned out, she was quite successful at it too. Zoë has already won several prizes; once she was runner-up champion.

Zoë threw a party to celebrate her 25th anniversary in the family. The family offered her a nice hi-fi chain and a collection of CDs. In summer time the foster father usually works in the garden until 8 p.m. When her foster father is not in, Zoë watches TV in the living room downstairs. When Maurice comes inside early, in winter time, she goes to her room upstairs to watch TV. She never sits together with her foster father in the evening. She is absolutely addicted to the current Flemish soaps. Zoë refuses to discuss her finances and savings with Maurice, and is even quite secretive about them.

The foster father tells us that as a young lad he had always been deeply shocked by the appalling conditions in which some boarders used to live. "Their clothes were of a very bad quality, beyond imagination," as he recalls. "They wore no shoes, only clogs; women wore dresses made of rough, stiff linen. I swore I would do something about this when I grew up. Compared to the past, they are now 'ladies and gentlemen'," he smiles.

Zoë was a boarder in a number of other foster families before coming "home". Things did not quite work out there, but the chemistry with her present family was right immediately. She has now spent 28 years here without serious problems. "My mother allowed her to do as she pleased," Maurice explains, "and that strategy was successful. Zoë is the boss and she relishes that role!" Every Thursday she cleans the house on her own initiative and does not need any supervision. Maurice helps her program the electric washing machine, but that is the extent of the assistance required. Zoë takes care of the rest. She sleeps very well at night.

Her family never visits. Long time ago, her mother, a pipe-smoking lady, paid her a visit, just once. Zoë no longer seems to care about her family. She calls her foster father by his Christian name, as if he were a brother. Zoë goes abroad on vacation together with a number of OPZ friends. Zoë does not only attend dance classes, she also practises various sports, like volleyball. She is proud to have been on TV twice. Zoë now understands that some of her former foster families used to exploit her. At one of these places she had to sleep in the barn with the pigs to assist sows giving birth, while the farmer was sound asleep in his bed. She also had to lift really heavy bails of straw and such. As a young girl Zoë attended what she calls "boarding schools" in Antwerp and Namur. Every two years, Zoë is taken to the zoo in Antwerp by one of her girlfriends. The OPZ withdraws approximately $35, so she can pay for this trip. Zoë admits that she is elegantly dressed, "that she looks nice", whenever she goes out.

2005

As I visited in 2005, I was confronted with some adversities. Fortunately, things have taken a turn for the better now. Zoë had needed knee surgery twice. The first time she was in hospital for three weeks; the second time she was there for all of four months. So Maurice was forced to cook his own meals. A lot of variation there was not. He ate boiled potatoes and bacon for lunch, and, in the evening, he had fried potatoes and bacon. "A healthy country meal, just like in the old days," Maurice stated.

Maurice fell a while ago and broke two vertebrae. He slept on the couch downstairs for a long time and ate his meals standing up, for he could not sit. He was flat on his back for roughly four months. He needed Zoë to help him put on his socks and shoes. To make matters worse, Rex, the neighbour's dog and Zoë's best friend, died. When the neighbour, a single man himself, had been taken into hospital, his children had brought his dog to a kennel. A week later it had died. "It couldn't cope with its loss," Maurice offered.

But life can be kind as well. A professional film crew was in and out of the house to film Zoë's and Maurice's life story. They couldn't watch the documentary, as they do not own a video player, but their neighbours were very obliging: they let them watch the documentary in their home. Zoë was over the moon. The film has won an important award at an international festival in the meantime. The film shows a year in the life of three families and uses the theme of the four seasons. Vivaldi's music resounds in the background and creates the right atmosphere. Zoë feels flattered and imagines herself to be quite an actress. It has always given her immense pleasure to be considered a fancy lady when going out.

Zoë no longer breeds rabbits and hamsters, even though she stills owns a few. Her activities have shifted to another domain. Every morning she visits a lonely neighbour. The man can hardly get about and waits to be admitted to a home. She lends him a hand and makes sure he has everything he needs for the day. Zoë, who has turned 60 recently, still does all the shopping without a shopping list. When she needs loads of stuff, she has a friend accompany her. Zoë's troubles with her knee haven't stopped her really. She picked up where she left off. She still goes out in weekends. She visits local pubs. The OPZ club for patients is wasted on her. She dresses up and gets a lot of pleasure out of people commenting on her looks and fancy clothes. Her previous interest in the other sex has somewhat diminished over the years.

Comment

As we understand it, Zoë is the very impersonation of a fully rehabilitated person. In spite of her limited intellectual capacity and language skills, she manages on her own. She is appreciated and feels needed. "I am a housewife," she smiles. Both at home and in the neighbourhood she is completely accepted as "one of them", even though everyone is aware of her link with the Hospital. Her foster father and the district nurse discretely keep an eye on her.

6) Child in the picture

2000

As usual, we enter the house by the back door in the company of the district nurse. The traffic in the area is congested. In a corner of the living room a 17-year-old boy, the son of the house, and his girlfriend are chatting. A nine-year-old girl, the boy's sister, is sitting with them. The foster mother, Agnes, is in her forties. She takes us to another corner of the room to talk. While we are discussing the Geel system, the youngsters join us for a while, then leave again. Somewhat later the foster father, a retired farmer in his sixties, enters the room. There are two male patients in the household, Jan (68) and Alfred (72). The foster mother has also been taking care of her demented mother-in-law for seven years now.

The foster mother states: "Life is not always easy but one must take it as it comes." She adds that foster families must include their patients in all aspects of family life, so that they can participate like the other members of the household. She stresses that her patients are treated well and have a nice time.

Jan and Alfred are both senior people. Quite recently, the family had taken in a third, younger patient, a man in his mid-forties. However, it didn't take the family long to come to the conclusion that the latter didn't fit in. The patient used to come downstairs in the morning only dressed in his bathrobe, "while we a have a young daughter of nine in the house." The patient also demanded freshly laundered white trousers three times a week. "Clients of that sort can be hard to keep up with. Most of them have been alcohol or drug addicts at some stage, and are impossible to live with," the foster mother comments.

At the time of my first visit, Alfred was in hospital with a broken hip. The foster mother visited him several times a week. At the time of my second interview, Alfred was back home and looked well. The other patient, Jan, is a very popular character in Geel. The foster mother calls him "a smart loony". Jan knows everybody and is extremely well informed, but would not be able to live by himself. He doesn't want to be associated with the OPZ at all, and doesn't attend any event organized by the Hospital. "Not my thing!", he volunteers. He graciously declines the right to be taken by taxi to the club, like Alfred. As a soccer fan, he cheers on two clubs. He also loves fishing in the pond behind the house. From time to time his foster father invites him to a fishing party in the Netherlands. Jan refuses to enrol in the OPZ fishing club. When the parents go out—which happens from time to time—Jan is left in charge. Dutifully, he looks after the demented grandmother. He does not let anybody in, and never disappoints.

During one of our visits, Jan comes in and joins us. All of a sudden, Anouk, nine years old at that time, takes him by the hand and leads him to the kitchen and veranda. They soon return and show us some drawings of a house, a church, a garden, and a few other sheets of paper with sums and figures. "These are examples of Jan's daily homework," the foster mother explains. No sooner has the young lady come home from school, than she puts Jan and Alfred to work. She teaches them what she has been taught at school, mostly in sessions of more than an hour. Alfred is not able to perform his tasks, but is expected to sit still and keep quiet. Jan is a good pupil. (Standing behind his "teacher", he winks at us, while she shows off the results of his efforts.) Jan has developed an excellent joking relationship with his foster mother. They tease each other constantly.

The foster mother is happy with the allowance she receives: about 2,580 US dollars every four months. The money is tax-free. The family grows its own vegetables and raises its own animals in the backyard, a remnant of what used to be a farm. This reduces the cost of boarding. In the course of our first meeting, the foster mother tells me twice that quite a number of big farmers used to enrich themselves by exploiting the work of the "sick", and that they still refuse to acknowledge this. Alfred, e.g., spent many years of his life toiling on a farm.

2005

During our visit in 2005, we learned that Jan had died about four years previously. Anouk had found it hard to come to terms with his death. Alfred too has gone. As he could no longer manage due to a bad hip, he was taken into care in the OPZ. The foster mother still visits with Alfred every so often and the relationship has remained quasi intact. Agnes took in another guest, a fairly old man, but he didn't stay long. He found it hard to adjust to the family. According to his foster mother, he intentionally soiled himself; he sometimes refused to eat and he stood outside for hours on end, even though it was freezing. Sometimes he put on two coats, but outside he went.

Even though the foster mother is currently struggling with some health problems herself, she adopted a new patient, a 40-year-old woman. Mia, as she is called, hasn't quite settled yet; both parties still have to get used to one another. The foster mother finds it difficult to cope with the guest's urge for independence. Mia can be quite affectionate towards her foster mother, but she apparently has no intention to be "one of them". When she comes home at night after her day's work, she barely stays in to finish her tea. She disappears into the night on her bike. In addition she is quite secretive about what she does, where she goes, etc. Having accidentally bumped into Mia in a pub in the company of a married man, her foster mother got suspicious. She finds it hard to trust Mia despite her kind words. Mia and Anouk do not seem to bond either.

Agnes wonders if the OPZ should continue to place similar patients in families. The latter aspire independence, and are less inclined to settle in the family. "They see us as a hotel," Agnes complains. The foster parents get frustrated, since they are worried about their patient and feel unhappy in their relationship with their boarder. "Bonding" is inherent in the Geel tradition and does not take place in some cases.

Comment

The affective and authentic bond built on trust between the two old men and the little girl stands out in this case. The contrast between the family's past and present experience is quite striking.

7) A son of the family*

2000

The foster mother, Martha (80), lost her husband ten years ago. Her guest, François (62) arrived in the family when he had just turned seventeen. According to Martha, he was more than welcome and it didn't take them long to treat him like their son: "He was the child we never had." Martha merely continued her family's tradition. It wasn't a big step for her since both sets of grandparents and her parents had always had guests. Like her predecessors, she and her husband were farmers. Martha and François still live in the old farmhouse.

François is francophone by origin. That's why we started conversing in French. His French was excellent, but it wasn't long before François switched to Flemish. François was sent to Geel from a poorhouse. He sees himself as an adopted child, and is adamant he is "not a guy from the Colony". Even so, during my second visit he spontaneously offered to show his OPZ booklet to me. Every year he goes to Spain with the OPZ, and he was the president of the patients' sports club for a long time. He is all too aware that he is an OPZ patient, but he hates being reminded of this and represses the idea. Although he considers himself as a son of the family, he never calls Martha "mother". He invariably uses her first name, or jokingly refers to her as "our madam".

In the past, François worked side by side with his foster father on the farm. The latter quickly discovered that "orders" were wasted on François and that a different approach was necessary if he wanted François to do any work at all. So his foster father let him set his own tasks, and that seemed to work all right. François would even take on the odd job from outsiders. As the story goes, at one stage he accepted to do some gardening for one of the OPZ psychiatrists. Having the impression that François' weeding wasn't quite up to scratch, the lady of the manor told him that she expected "to see black earth only" when she returned. In no time at all François had cut all the flowers. He had then proceeded to extract all the plants. The result was a basically barren garden, reduced to black earth indeed, and a totally flabbergasted psychiatrist. François argued, that he had done nothing but obey her orders. "It is hopeless," sighed Martha, "he does not want to take orders from anybody. He even disregards

* cf. DVD

Cycling means the world to François
(Photo E. Roosens)

his own district nurse and psychiatrist!" When his foster mother had asked him to put on a clean shirt for my benefit, his answer had allegedly been quite rude. As it turned out, François came in to see me in his overalls, straight out of the garden.

"He is as free as a bird!", exclaims his mother. When at home, François is as sloppy as they come. "Our Blackie," Martha calls him. But when he goes out on weekends, he seems quite a different fellow. He dresses up and takes pride in his appearance. In his younger years, François managed to decline the kind services of the OPZ's "travelling teacher". In the end this gentleman gave up, exasperated. Whenever the teacher visited, François would hasten to prepare lunch and invite the teacher to join him. As a result no teaching was ever done. The only lesson he had ever accepted was writing his signature, a skill that, as the president of his sports club, he badly needed. It took "a few years of Martha's life" to teach him that.

François rides his bicycles quite a lot. He has four bikes, one of which is a racing bike. He is also the proud owner of a tandem. François uses the tandem for his weekend trips with his girl friend: "She does not know traffic regulations, she turns to the right or the left as she pleases without looking!" François also participates in sports camps, and is often away from home. He never misses a vacation in the Mediterranean. Ibiza was a bit of a disappointment, however: "This place has nothing to offer: a pile of stones, that's about it. I toured the island on a bicycle in just one day!", he pouted. "Now Benidorm, that's a different story!"

"He is good company, he really is! I thoroughly enjoy it!", says his mother. François is doing the garden all by himself and nobody is allowed to interfere. He is the boss, no doubt about that. As soon as Martha appears to have a look at his work, he tells her to go away. "You see all of this? He owns it!", Martha jokes.

François talks fluently and is very much at ease and uninhibited; he is full of humour. Black humour mostly. At our second visit he remarked: "I cannot die, for the simple reason that I have already been dead twice!", alluding to the fact that he had a near-death-experience twice.

"François grabs whatever cash he can get his hands on." He steals, and later vehemently denies having done so. He does all the shopping for the household, but Martha makes him advance the money and later reimburses him. His foster parents have tried their best to eradicate his kleptomania for years on end, but to no avail. "He is not in Geel for sweaty feet!", she sighs. "When he arrived here as a youngster, he was ever so pale. He was underfed, to say the least. He couldn't even push a wheelbarrow and was always tired." François suffered from terrible backaches and his performance as a farm aid was way below average. Not even half of what one would normally expect. The doctor prescribed lots of cycling as a cure, and this turned out to be a good remedy. The backaches gradually disappeared. At present, at the age of 62, François still plays soccer.

In former days, François used to drink a lot and this could trigger aggressive behaviour. "I will kill them all! I will slice their throat!", were some of his favourite outcries; but fortunately, he never acted on his words. His foster parents managed to gradually get his drinking problem under control. He still visits pubs, but doesn't necessarily get plastered anymore.

After the death of her husband, Martha was asked if François could stay. As she had never experienced problems with him and had never felt menaced, she said yes. François had developed an outspoken joking relationship with his late foster father and their relationship was excellent. "François is able to outtalk anybody!", his mother muses. François is both witty and manipulative.

François has a half-brother and a sister. Even so, he has never received a visit. "Should my mother stop by, I wouldn't hesitate to show her the door!", François says quick as a flash. François boasts that he has "lots of money", and that he loves the idea of being rich. Mathematics aren't his forte, however. He can add up to some extent, but that's all. At night, François expects Martha to go to bed first. He personally locks all the doors and stays up as long as it suits him. Mostly he watches television.

2005

As I revisit the family in 2005, I could tell they had both sailed through some rough seas over the past few years. Martha had taken a serious fall about 18 months previously. François was in Crete at the time, so he wasn't around when it all happened. Upon his return he was forced to stay in the OPZ as there was nobody at home. As a result of the fall, Martha can barely walk. To this day she needs physiotherapy. To make things worse, François was hit by a car just before Christmas 2004. "Her ladyship (the driver) was on her bloody phone," François acidly remarks. He was extremely upset because it meant he couldn't look after Martha. During his weeklong stay in the hospital, she was admitted to a retirement home, as she could not manage on her own. Both have become co-dependent in their old age.

According to some, François has gone downhill bit by bit over the past few years, particularly since his accident. He no longer plays soccer. He has lost interest in his garden. He has given up the presidency of the sports club. He himself alleges he has quite simply retired. His view doesn't concur with other people's views: "I am not going downhill, quite on the contrary, I am making progress from where I am standing!"

François rightfully points out that he has become "Madam's" guardian angel: "I put her to bed and only then dare I leave. The dog will bark if I am needed." A part-time carer has been cooking and cleaning for them, for years now. It is François, though, who answers the phone since Martha's hearing is increasingly impaired. And it is François who helps Martha get about in the house. François has gotten over his cycling phobia, which means he can quickly alert the neighbours should it be necessary. Rumour has it, that both François and Martha are about to be admitted to a retirement home. They will inhabit a unit by themselves, but will be able to get assistance whenever necessary.

Quite remarkably, both their sense of humour and their mutual joking relationship have remained intact. Even so, having observed them closely, it is easy to see the bantering between mother and son disguises a deep concern. Martha secretly hopes François will not survive her by long: "It would be such a disaster if they were to put him in a home." François on the other hand keeps confirming that Martha is doing really well: "Martha has a strong heart. Martha has a 95-year-old sister, so Martha, who is merely 85, has years to go. You should go and play tennis," he jokes to Martha.

François has suggested to his district nurse, that he could perfectly manage on his own if it were to come to that. The nurse thinks that is not an option. Never does the mutual concern about each other's future lead to self-pity though. They are always in high spirits, the tone of the conversation remains optimistic. François boasts that he smokes like a chimney, ignoring Martha's ongoing protests: "I do not smoke, I have told the doctor time and time again. I puff." Upon which Martha remarks: "He won't quit, not even for me!" François takes pride in his collection of bikes. He let me take his picture in front of the house in the company of his favourite bike. Every Saturday and Sunday he cycles to his pub, not the OPZ clubhouse near the station. "No true friendship to be had there," he remarks.

But all is not gloom. Like Maurice and Zoë, Martha and François were followed by film-maker Arnout Hauben for the better part of a year. They truly enjoyed it. They too received a videotape of the documentary, but like the others they did not manage to watch it at home. As a matter of fact, François does not own a video player. As soon as they came on the market, he purchased a DVD-player. In the spring 2006, the documentary was shown to the general public in Geel. All sessions were immediately sold out. People in Geel and surrounding towns clearly identify with traditional foster family care and are proud to be part of it all. Press coverage was unanimous in its appreciation.

In 2005 François celebrated his 50th anniversary in Geel. He spent this entire period in one single family. The celebration took place in the local parish hall and was attended by quite a few VIPs and journalists. Articles appeared in both a local and a regional newspaper. François still keeps up with soccer on TV and knows everything there is to know about the corruption scandals that have recently been exposed. "If it weren't for soccer, TV would be a complete and utter waste of time," according to François. He still attends live matches as well. Martha is quite sure that young people will continue the tradition of foster family care. François doesn't share that view: "The young ones do not want to stay at home, they want to travel." "If 'Madam' is still around, you are more than welcome to visit again," François said as I bade farewell. "And if I am not, he is welcome in your home, isn't he?", Martha replied.

8) An informed decision

2000

A very roomy, as good as new, trendy house built in one of Geel's hamlets. Roger (40) and his wife Rita (40) didn't become foster parents at whim. They gave it much thought. Roger is a skilled technician employed by a major international company and Rita is a nurse. She knows the Geel system inside out. The foster family has four young children. Rita's mother hosts an OPZ guest as well.

Three female patients are currently living in the family: Trui (82), Germaine (70) and Vera (53). Vera works in a sheltered workshop at the OPZ. The two other guests are always at home. A professional journal published an extensive report on this family in 1998. According to the foster parents, living with patients isn't rewarding from a financial point of view. Life is quite enjoyable though.

Trui is from Holland. She sits in her favourite chair all day long; she usually knits. She does not like the children to come too close when playing. She lives in her own world. Vera is seriously ill. Contact with her is difficult. She is obsessed with cigarettes. She is married. Her children have been taken into care, some of them live in sheltered accommodation. One of her children visits her from time to time. Vera does not eat much. She is just hanging around. She constantly walks in and out in order to light yet another cigarette. Vera is completely shut off from reality. Nothing seems to touch her anymore. On Sundays, she takes a cab and leaves for the patients' club. She has two boyfriends: one for the morning and one for the afternoon. These men donate cigarettes, which seems to be their only purpose. Vera stems from a family with a long history of appalling problems and tragedies. Her own household didn't fare any better. Her children and grandchildren followed in her tracks. Vera visits one of her sisters every month. She looks forward to it every single time. This sister is the only person who has stayed loyal to her. She remains grateful that Vera raised her after their mother had died in childbirth. As hygiene is increasingly problematic, Vera may have to return to the Hospital, maybe for good.

Germaine lives by the clock. Every evening she goes up to her room to watch television. She loves soaps and enjoys listening to music. Germaine owns state-of-the-art equipment. Every night she goes to bed at 10.30 p.m. sharp. During one of our visits, Germaine barged in, interrupted our conversation and signalled to her foster mother that it was time to eat. She seemed quite anxious. Routine is extremely important to her, especially when food is concerned. Every Saturday afternoon and Sunday, Germaine cycles to the centre of Geel. Germaine makes trips with her boyfriend. She feels most at ease with small children who do not outsmart her. She likes to cuddle them too. Germaine's native tongue is French but she commands Flemish. She annually spends a week in Spain. She also attends sports camps and goes on day-trips. She refuses to work at the OPZ though. Germaine is always overstimulated when she returns from her Sunday trips. Her foster parents feel that Germaine has grown more independent. "Too much so!", they complain.

Roger and Rita estimate that the allowance foster parents receive should be reconsidered. They are satisfied with what they have got, but they feel it is the absolute minimum. They took their time before becoming foster parents and built their house with that plan in mind. I was invited to visit all three patient rooms. They are spacious and comfortable.

Both foster parents fear that some mental institutions refrain from sending patients to Geel, even though the latter may be much better off in Geel where they get a chance to live in society. Although the Geel system has considerably improved over the past decade, Roger and Rita admit they would appreciate closer involvement of the psychiatrist and psychologist. The latter could help foster families deal with the problems they face on a daily basis. More contact between the professionals and foster parents may also prevent some mismatches. Mismatches damage both the persons involved and the Hospital's image, according to the couple: "People are sometimes left with the impression that all patients are hard to handle these days." The children of the family are perfectly attuned to the presence of the three patients. "We get on like a house on fire," says the 13-year-old son.

2005

In 2005 the situation is pretty much the same. The kids have aged of course. The older boy is at college now; the younger boy has just turned 10. In the meantime the family has "adopted" the paternal grandmother as she became physically unwell. She lives in a studio. The kids really enjoy having so many people around. Nothing seems to have changed for Trui who recently turned 87. Germaine currently works at the OPZ, as does Vera. Trui has the house all to herself during the working week.

No sooner have we walked in, than we all start talking about the foster family care system and its future. The foster parents feel that the OPZ sometimes tries to place patients in families who really do not belong there; people who do not want to be a part of the family. They would rather be free, which basically amounts to the fact that they are inconsiderate and do not take the family into account. They merely want to do as they please. They refuse to integrate in the family, they are absent as much as they can. There is no bonding. Families feel increasingly frustrated. It is no secret that the Geel system cannot cope with just any psychiatric patient. The foster parents continue: "People eventually start caring about each other; this is the very strength of the system. If a relationship of some sort is not possible, a placement is doomed to fail." In the couple's view, failure is a sure thing when patients behave like guests in a hotel. The family is then reduced to being a sort of landlord. The problem, as the family sees it, is that the "landlord" still feels responsible for his guest. This responsibility is particularly hard to bear if one has no impact at all on the guest's behaviour. This is untenable in the long run. Some sort of shared values and structure are vital.

Comment

Amongst foster parents, one finds a few young people with college degrees—a minority admittedly—who critically reflect on the evolution of the Geel system. They think things over carefully and know how to argue their case. Rita and Roger know what they are talking about; they are insiders who have totally committed to the foster family care system. They are prepared to fight for their cause. As should be apparent from some other family portraits we have painted, others share their views. It needs to be said that the current OPZ management actively encourages people to state their views. It is more than willing to yield the floor to these people and involve them in the decision-making process.

9) An absorbing daughter

2000

A middle-class house. When I first visited, the foster mother, Germaine, edging on 60, received me all by herself. Her husband was out on business and her foster daughter was working at the OPZ. A second interview took place in similar conditions. The guest, Aline (52), wouldn't take kindly to being asked to stay home and forego work. She very rigidly sticks to her daily routines. When she needs to stay home on weekdays for some reason or other, she is very anxious and unsettled. Aline also refuses to go shopping with her foster mother on weekdays. She can only be persuaded to do so on weekends.

Aline is not able to administer her own money and does not know how to count, although she can tell a piece of 20 BEF[9], which she calls “a brownie”, from a piece of 5 BEF, which she calls “a red”. But that is about it. She does not touch her pocket money and refuses to spend her own funds. If she learns, for instance, that the toothpaste in her room has been paid for with her own money, she will not use it. She only consumes things that are financed by somebody else. She wants to save every last penny she owns.

Aline’s photographs show a neat and carefully dressed lady. Not a trace of mental problems of any kind. Aline arrived in the family at the age of 15, 37 years ago. At that time, her foster parents were living together with Germaine’s parents as an extended kin group. They all continued to live together for another seven years after Aline’s arrival. Both Germaine’s parents and maternal grandparents used to foster. Germaine’s father was a carpenter, her mother a shopkeeper. Germaine’s husband, on the other hand, didn’t grow up amongst patients.

Aline is francophone by birth but learned Flemish, the latter being her first language now. She was badly neglected by her family and still feels rejected by them. A suitcase that she brought when she first came to Geel still reminds her of her family. She says that it belonged to her brother and doesn’t want it in her room. Her last contact with a close relative took place about 32 years ago. Not for lack of trying. Wanting to re-establish a relationship with Aline’s brother, Germaine wrote to him. He never responded. Aline is not able to read the clock and uses the sun as her guide. When the sun rises, it is time to go to work. Interestingly, Aline can tell weekends from other days. At home she is in charge of the dog and the chickens which she feeds twice a day. But sometimes she forgets to do so.

The foster parents have two sons. One son is married. Aline figures on one of his wedding photos. She has always been very friendly to the children, and is similarly sweet towards the grandchildren. She calls her foster mother “mummy”, “mother” or “Germaine”. Occasionally, Aline accompanies her foster parents on a shopping expedition; but she often finds this upsetting. They need to reassure her and calm her down. When she is trying on clothes, she doesn’t feel comfortable and starts to sweat, which makes her increasingly anxious.

At the age of 15, Aline had a serious drinking problem. She secretly drank part of a considerable stock of wine and beer from a deceased relative of the foster family, a wine dealer. Having emptied the bottles, she skilfully placed back the corks. She managed to keep her drinking habit hidden for months on end. Once unmasked, it took her four years to overcome her addiction. “Our guests need a lot of support but eventually they manage,” her foster mother commented in a matter-of-fact tone when questioned about this episode.

Aline is not on good terms with all the family members. Not everybody was invited to the dinner party in honour of her 50th birthday. She did invite her boyfriend Rudy though. He is a co-patient who has been her fiancé for a long time now. Aline has her own personal mug,

9 BEF = Belgian frank (40.4 BEF = 1 EURO).

a present from Rudy. She sees Rudy every day at the OPZ workshop. They kiss when the supervisor isn't looking. Rudy seems to be a very loyal partner. He buys Aline presents all year round. Quite exceptionally, she reciprocates by offering him a pullover, for example. In Aline's world this state of affairs is normal. She is not faithful. She is firmly convinced that she is entitled to more than one fiancé. She tries to get in touch with older men whenever she can. Her foster mother thinks she may be looking for a father figure: "Maybe, she desperately misses her dad?" In her family of origin, Aline was badly treated. She did not have a bed and was forced to sleep on the floor. Food was scarce, beer readily available. One of her aunts, who paid her a visit a long time ago, mentioned gruesome details about the poor kid's youth. Some days, Aline refuses to accompany her foster parents when they go out for lunch. She loves to have the place all to herself, and on these occasions she wanders through the entire house. The married son, who lives in the neighbourhood, keeps an eye on the house whenever Aline is there on her own.

Aline used to play a lot with her dolls and bears, and even now she is fond of puzzles for children and children's programmes on television, like *The Teletubbies*. Aline usually watches television in the family room, although she has her own TV in her bedroom. She does not like her own set because its screen is too small. Her favourite music is the *lambada*. If no partner is available, Aline dances by herself. She has a good sense of rhythm and truly enjoys dancing at parties. Aline cannot write. Until recently she spent her holidays in Spain or France; more recently she has started going to the Belgian coast with a group of older and less mobile patients.

At night, Aline suffers from panic attacks and nightmares. She sees the grim Reaper standing at the foot of her bed. When haunted by these fantasies, she presses against the wall and howls. One night she tried to send the grim Reaper to an aged family member she didn't like. The rationale being that the latter was old while she was still young, so the former deserved to die more. Aline refuses to grow old. The day she first heard about cremation she was absolutely horrified. According to Aline, death usually seizes her from behind. When she dies, she expects her foster parents to order a plane. She has given them explicit instructions. The plane must land in the backyard and then take her to heaven, or to her friend, "Johnny-the-Moon". At night, Aline leaves her curtains wide open so she can look at her friend "Johnny-the-Moon", even when he does not show up right away. He might just appear in the middle of the night, and she does not want to miss him.

When she was younger, Aline got really bossy every so often. She harangued the children, shouting: "Who is the boss, here? You or me? I have been living with mother much longer than you have, haven't I?" Fortunately, these outbursts were rather exceptional. Aline still gets in that mood from time to time. Recently, she told the married son who happened to pop in: "You, stay here, will you! You have been married long enough!" When Aline is told that the family is considering a second patient, her response is quite sharp: "Really? See if I care! I will show her how to take care of the dog and the chickens, and I will keep an eye on her!"

Sometime ago, while retaining Rudy as her fiancé, Aline set eyes on a male patient in the neighbourhood. She even tried "to find" money at her foster parent's home to buy him cigarettes. Rudy cried like a baby when he learned that "Aline had taken another lover". Rudy is only a bit more mature than Aline, but contrary to his beloved, he has values he lives by.

Germaine hopes that foster care in Geel will be continued, but fears it might not. Her married son, e.g., would like to take in a patient, but his wife doesn't. Foster care is not a source of real income these days. Take Aline for example. To her as to many other patients, eating is tremendously important. She is the one who decides on the menu: mussels, crab salad, steak tartar, etc., all rather expensive items. She enjoys eating and really appreciates it, but the allowance foster parents receive does not cover fancy food. Aline's foster mother has never calculated the actual cost, but she is pretty sure that she loses money by giving Aline what she asks for. "But we miss her dearly when she is away on vacation!", she quickly adds. Germaine honours the wise words of her own father: "If you had handicapped children yourself, you would want them to be well treated. Take care of your guests as if they were your own sons and daughters."

2005

When I visited in 2005, the foster parents report Aline hasn't changed much. She is still involved with Rudy. She has totally lost interest in the chickens though. The foster father, who used to be a welder, has retired, so he is around a lot more.

In the meantime the foster parents acted on their plans and took in a second client. Her name is Pia. She arrived in November 2004. According to the foster parents, Aline and Pia get along just fine. Germaine had assumed that a second and relatively young female client would have a positive effect on her own workload in the household, but that turned out to be wishful thinking. At the initial meeting, Pia said exactly the right things. She didn't act on her words, though. Pia turns out to have a knack for manipulating. She manages to have other members of the family take over her chores. By day she works in the OPZ workshop. It is hard for her to learn very simple tasks like folding T-shirts. Positive is that she is very affectionate: she kisses and hugs her foster mother and does apologize when she feels she has made a mistake. In that sense she is a perfectly acceptable housemate.

Towards the end of the interview, Pia came in. She was dropped off by one of the OPZ drivers. She had been in hospital for treatment. One can tell from the way she looks at people that she is a bit retarded. Pia spontaneously brought up her past. She comes out of a family with 16 children, of whom 11 are still alive. Her father used to sell newspapers and also worked as a gravedigger. Both her parents died young. One of her older brothers was appointed her legal guardian. One night, this brother, in a rash mood, bragged in a pub about "lots of money" he allegedly had on him. Upon leaving the pub, he was followed by two men who robbed him and left him for dead. Pia ended up in an institution. She worked in a sheltered accommodation for 23 years before coming to Geel. She wrapped stuff for a pharmaceutical company and a jam factory. In the OPZ workshop Pia does not fit in; she doesn't get along with the others.

The future of the family care programme is brought up towards the end of our talk. The foster parents are of the opinion the allowances are on the low side. The OPZ has allegedly promised that some extra money would come their way. Sadly, nothing has come of that. At the same time the foster parents admonish, that paying too much money would be counterproductive also. Some might only do it for the money! According to Germaine, there are still a few families—she had one particular family in mind—who do not treat their patient right.

10) A very possessive son

2000

An old farm. The nurse accompanies me to the back door while an immense and aggressive dog is barking and jumping up and down its kennel. In the over-heated kitchen, Gertrude, 89 (she looks more like 75) and a tiny man in his early 70s, Mieleke, are eagerly awaiting our visit. Mieleke is wearing a blue duster. Mieleke arrived in Gertrude's family 40 years ago. To break the ice, the nurse jokes that Mieleke wants everything to happen on time: rising in the morning, breakfast, lunch, dinner, television. He adds that he could make an excellent contribution to the Belgian Railways by having trains run on time. Mieleke has no ears for this kind of humour. Actually he does not care for visitors. Not even Gertrude's granddaughter. "He would rather see the back of her!", Gertrude comments.

The foster mother grew up among boarders. There were twelve children in the family, nine of them are still alive. They all live in Geel and all of them host patients. None of them have ever had problems with boarders. Gertrude started fostering in 1934. She has never had to send a boarder back to the OPZ. The foster mother, who has a sharp wit and looks incredibly optimistic, bought a new car two years ago, at the age of 87. Only recently has she stopped driving.

Gertrude is talking to Mieleke in a soft and motherly tone. Miel is doing all the shopping for the household in the nearby supermarket, where they call him "Mister Miel". At night, Miel expects his mother to go to bed first. He switches off the lights and carefully locks up the house. According to his foster mother, Miel has improved considerably since he arrived. At first he was not able to do anything. His own mother had washed and dressed him until he was 20. When he arrived at his foster home, he did not dare use a knife at the dinner table. He is much more capable now, but wants everything to happen on time. A strict routine is essential. Dinner is at 4 p.m., TV starts at 6 p.m., and bedtime is at 9 p.m. sharp. This time schedule must be closely adhered to, lest Mieleke gets "nervous".

Mieleke is exceptionally jealous and, as already said, does not tolerate visitors. Even so, he did accept the presence of another boarder who was already living in the family when he arrived. He even learned a lot from this older colleague. This co-patient died some years ago. Mieleke was not willing to accept a new co-boarder. When one day a candidate was introduced, Mieleke worked him out of the house by means of a broom. "He wants to have me all to himself," his foster mother explains, "he must be the one and only, just like a child."

After he had left the room for a few moments, fetching a newspaper, his foster mother asked me not to enquire about her age or to even allude to it, as it might upset Mieleke. He might get scared, and run away. He cannot handle anything that makes him think about the advanced age of his mother. He knows that she is very old and that one day she will disappear, but he can not face this reality. I try to avoid any allusion to aging, but twice I inadvertently refer to a date of the past, and twice Mieleke jumps up from his chair and intends to run off. His mother calls him back, however, and orders him to sit: "This gentleman has not asked any questions about 'it'!", she says, without specifying what this "it" means. Before coming to Geel, Miel had been employed by Catholic brothers in a pilgrimage resort.

Miel reads a lot, whatever he can lay his hands on: newspapers and magazines of all kinds. Every Sunday he attends mass. In the afternoon he faithfully visits the museum of the Old Hospital and the Saint Dimpna church. For those occasions Miel wears a formal suit and tie. One Sunday we happened to meet him in the museum. He just looked like the other visitors, only his hat and woollen winter suit on a hot summer day gave him away. In 1997, the local newspaper published an article on him, the museum's most loyal visitor. His photo appeared on the front page. Miel treasures this issue. He is attached to churches, bishops, priests, etc. and refuses to watch most soap operas on television "as they are immoral". Miel has a large collection of books and magazines in his bedroom. He memorizes all possible events including their exact date and time. On Sundays, Miel has a beer in a few pubs too. "He is not ye typical OPZ lad!", his mother smiles. In wintertime, when it is cold, Mieleke stays home on Sundays and treats himself to half a bottle of wine.

Miel has a brother who picks him up for a week's vacation every year. Occasionally they drive to the brother's villa in Germany. Miel does not like Germany however: people speak another language and it is often cold over there.

2005

In 2005, the foster mother had died sometime ago. Mieleke was still living in the same house, but under the guardianship of Gertrude's son and his partner. The district nurse is optimistic: "Mieleke is doing just fine. He sticks to his rather rigid routine and copes as best he can." I didn't feel it would be a good idea, to go and see Mieleke now that he had lost his foster mother. It might bring back memories and upset him. He has a very good memory, so the chance that my visit would distress him was far too high.

Comment

Since his arrival in the family 40 years ago, Mieleke has changed beyond recognition. At first he was not able to do anything at all, he was scared and anxious all the time. Gradually he evolved, be it within the boundaries of a safe world by his own design. He was always encouraged and supported by Gertrude who watched over him with a smile.

11) Two daughters to be

2000

A house in a rural part of Geel. Both foster parents, Jan and Elvire, are 60. They became foster parents in 1968, after they had built their new five-bedroom house. The family has three children. At the beginning of his career, Jan walked out of the house at 5.30 a.m. every morning to return no earlier than 7 p.m. The family not only took in patients to have some help around the house, but also to keep Elvire company. Later on, the foster mother got a part-time job which she kept for many years. At present, two female patients, Isabelle and Laura, are living there. They haven't quite settled in yet, but their integration in the family is well under way. Jan and Elvire had two other patients previously.

Isabelle (50) is from Wallonia. According to her foster mother, she behaves like a child and demands a lot of attention. She knows the value of the various banknotes but is not able to manage her own budget. She runs small errands only, for instance buying bread in a nearby shop. Her relatives never visit. Her 13-year-old daughter dropped in on her birthday, but they started quarrelling and the girl ran off. Isabelle's son has never called, nor has her husband who lives in Geel but has nothing to do with the Hospital. Legally, Isabelle is still his wife. Isabelle grew up in a family that was involved in prostitution. She didn't go to school and can neither read nor write. She was forced to run the household at a very tender age.

During the week Isabelle works at the OPZ workshop. She fears, without cause, that one day she will have to leave her present foster family, and implores her mother repeatedly not to send her away. Isabelle's imagination often runs wild. She lacks a realistic view of the world. She is a compulsive liar, although her foster mother presses her to always speak the truth. She also steals her own medication and cigarettes, even though the foster mother carefully hides them. Isabelle is only allowed eight cigarettes a day. When she is alone, she searches high and low for cigarettes. Isabelle moves about swiftly and inaudibly. Some days she rises at 6 a.m., makes coffee and lays the breakfast table. But that is about the only initiative she manages to take.

Isabelle used to have a boyfriend, but their relationship ended when the latter was seduced by another patient. She enjoys her work in the workshop and goes to Spain every year. Recently, she sneaked into her husband's home, but gave herself away by smuggling sausages of a particular brand back into her room, a regional specialty that is not readily available in Geel. On Sundays, Isabelle often visits Geel in the company of Laura. They travel by bus.

During our first visit, Laura (50) entered the room. She has some Black-African blood in her and it shows. When she first started working, the other patients referred to her as "the Negro". Laura was horrified and refused to return to the workshop. Laura, polite and fluent as she is, does not look like a mental patient. She helps with the household: she does the dishes, she dusts, she cleans the windows, etc. She is not a morning person, but once she gets going, she talks all day long. Before she came to Geel, she was about to get married. This is one of her favourite themes. Her family background is very problematic. However, Laura recently attended a family reunion. The happy occasion was her brother's birthday.

Both patients are strongly attached to their "dad" and "mom", and do not hesitate to cover their foster mother with kisses. When Laura and Isabelle go out on Sundays, they get together with their boyfriends and girlfriends. They obviously talk and giggle all day and have a jolly good time.

According to Laura, the quality of medication has remarkably improved over the last few years. Laura has learned a lot from her foster mother and misses her terribly when she is not around. A while ago her "mom" was in hospital and this truly distressed Laura. "They are ever so nice, they treat us like kings. If we feel like it, we can make toast even late at night!", Laura comments with her foster parents within earshot. Generally speaking, Laura is a likable person, although she is a real chatterbox. She doesn't like Mondays.

Before coming to Geel, Laura belonged to a sort of religious movement similar to the Jehova Witnesses. When she arrived in her foster family, she came with four bibles and regularly felt the urge to preach. Her foster parents weren't exactly thrilled with this kind of behaviour. One day, Laura surrendered her bibles to her foster mother, "who promptly proceeded to send them to heaven having consulted with Our Lady at Scherpenheuvel, a local place of pilgrimage." Parting with her bibles was a liberating experience for Laura. She felt enormously relieved. Her health improved instantly, she alleged. She is really happy now. When her foster mother spent some time in hospital, Laura felt very lonely and went to bed with a sculpture of Our Lady. Laura does not go to church on Sundays, but watches mass on TV.

At the time of our second visit, Laura was in France, on a pilgrimage to Our Lady of Lourdes. She has allegedly started writing an autobiography. Laura hates flying. That is why she never goes to Spain for her annual holiday. She frequently visits the family's daughter, who lives next-door. This daughter, a nurse, hosts Laura when her parents are on vacation. The foster parents assume that Laura is safeguarding her future by being particularly nice to their daughter: she hopes the daughter will take her in when they can no longer take care of her. Laura has even expressed the hope that her foster father will be the first "to go to heaven", as younger female patients are rarely left in the care of a widower. The foster parents informed us of this "plan" while Laura was not in.

Jan and Elvire estimate that boarders are much better off now than they used to be, but they fear that the young generation of Geelians is less inclined to take on the responsibility. This also applies to their own children. In young families both partners have a career.

Comment
This case illustrates how two patients who are radically different as to cultural background and personal history harmoniously live together in a foster family. They are like sisters. The fact that the foster parents belong to yet another subculture makes this successful cohabitation all the more special and remarkable. That her companions called her "the Negro" shocked Laura so much that she never set foot in that workshop again. At home, nobody seems to notice her being coloured. Laura feels perfectly accepted and at ease. She goes out on Sundays without much ado. It is as good as certain that Laura would be referred to as "Black", "Half-blooded" or "Negro"—categories with a negative connotation—in virtually any unsophisticated workplace in Flanders. Certainly in this area, coloured people, especially of Black-African descent, are not a common minority. So people aren't all that used to dealing with them.

2006
In 1999, both Isabelle and Laura obliged their foster parents. Both feared they might be sent back to the OPZ. The general atmosphere was positive. In seven years time things have significantly changed.

Isabelle now lives with another family. She increasingly revolted against her foster parents, ran away and often did not come home for the night. The police usually located her in her boyfriend's house, somewhere in Geel. In Spain too, when on holiday, her behaviour was unacceptable. In the family there was a lot of conflict between her and Laura, although Laura now claims she really misses Isabelle. She reminisces how much fun they used to have. They even devised a plan to escape together. Even though they never carried out this plan, they thoroughly enjoyed the secrecy surrounding the project. According to the foster parents, the relationship between the two ladies went up and down: sometimes it was excellent, other times it was hell. In the meantime Isabelle has expressed the wish to come back, but the foster family feels it wouldn't be right to acknowledge this request. Amongst other things they do not want to jeopardise the new foster parents' efforts to build a life together with Isabelle.

After a while Laura is invited to join our discussion. The first thing she says—tears streaming down her face—is that she is not happy in Geel and that she has never liked it. Even so, she adds that the only people she has ever cared about are her present foster parents and her brother. Still she would prefer to go back to an institution where she would be free to go out, have a boyfriend, have fun, dance, etc. Her foster mother remarks that Laura (51) is besotted with men.

Laura also states she is scared of small, confined spaces as well as of large spaces. That's why she no longer goes to church. The street too terrifies her: cars seem to come straight at her. She no longer wants to go to Scherpenheuvel, neither does she want to go to Lourdes (places of pilgrimage). She used to have an excellent relationship with the foster parents' daughter who lives next door with her family but that has come to an end too. At one point, Laura even hit this lady and that inevitably led to her being admitted to hospital. There is only one ray of hope in her life, i.e., the companionship of the grandson who lives next door. Laura takes him for walks, plays with him in the garden, she absolutely adores him. During our interview Laura repeated what she had said seven years previously: she had been about to get married when she got mental problems. As a consequence her fiancé had broken off the engagement. She had always wanted children, but that wish has never been fulfilled. According to her foster mother, Laura also dotes on the other grandchildren when they come for a visit.

Laura occasionally helps out around the house. Often she goes to her bedroom "to pray". She refuses to go and work at the OPZ because fellow patients might refer to her as "Negro". The foster mother says Laura isn't welcome anywhere as she causes conflict between people and behaves in an overly assertive or aggressive manner. The foster mother addresses Laura and says: "You are a real clown, you are, sometimes you are laughing and then out of the blue you start crying!" Tears welled up in Laura's eyes but then suddenly she burst into laugher. The foster parents find the relationship with Laura hard-going and the foster mother wonders whether she will be able to persevere. According to the foster mother, the OPZ staff isn't too keen on Laura either. She can be very difficult and even scolds the doctor who treats her. During our conversation, Laura keeps bursting out in tears and then, just as sudden, her face clears up and she smiles. The foster parents allege that the patients they used to have were easier to deal with. Their current guest is more brutal, she does as she pleases without taking her foster parents into account. They also feel that both Isabelle and Laura were more obliging the first few years, as they felt more insecure about their future. Once they got settled, they adopted a more uncompromising attitude.

Comment

Although roughly seven years ago a solid, mutual relationship between Laura, Isabelle and the foster family seemed well under way, it never materialised. Like others, these foster parents feel that the new generation of psychiatric patients is harder to deal with. The good old times when they had easygoing, affectionate patients seem to be well and truly over.

12) A terrible character, but one that belongs

2000

A contemporary house. Both foster parents are expecting us. Later on, a daughter and granddaughter join the conversation. The foster father, Karel (62), starts talking. He knows the system from within, from his childhood. His neighbours had always had guests. His grandfather, a small farmer, hosted patients as well. The foster mother, Angèle, who is from a neighbouring village, was not familiar with the system. That is why her husband first discarded the idea of taking in a boarder, but it was she who insisted, and eventually they committed. One of Angèle's aunts had encouraged her to start fostering as she was at home a lot.

Karel and Angèle have provided a home to several guests over the years. One of them, Alice (79), eventually returned to the Hospital after a 25-year stay in the family. Sadly, she had become too dependent and needy for Angèle to cope with. Alice wasn't able to speak, which Angèle described as a mixed blessing.

Another lady was called Suzy. She suffered from diabetes and was as good as blind. She was of Jewish origin. Suzy commanded several languages and was brilliant at mathematics; she used to help the children with their homework. She had a sister who lived in Switzerland, and a sister-in-law who was a famous singer. Suzy always planned everything to the minute: every hour of the day was accounted for, as were the number of steps she would take in the garden. Alice helped her make coffee and assisted Suzy with her daily "toilet". Suzy behaved very formally and addressed her foster parents with "Monsieur Charles" and "Madame Angèle".

Francine only stayed with the family for two years. She requested her own, personal chair at the table, collected stamps, and watched TV together with her foster parents. Her sister took her back to Antwerp; she now lives in sheltered accommodation. She was a very kind person, somewhat retarded, but not as isolated as many other patients.

Yet another patient, Sofie, went dancing in a local dancehall every week. And every time she fainted on the dance floor in order to attract attention. Her foster parents had to send her back to the Hospital as they could not handle her.

Their present patient, Sylvie, arrived in the family seventeen years ago. She is "very sick" and is on heavy tranquilizers. The foster father described her as a very selfish and unhygienic person, but "one of us" all the same. "Sylvie talks the legs of a wooden table." Watching television in Sylvie's company is not an option. She has her own TV but does not use it. When she returns from the OPZ workshop late afternoon, she always complains: "They have beaten me up! But, I am pretty, I am a real looker, aren't I?!" Sylvie gives away her lunch when it is not to her liking, and buys rice pudding or other treats at the OPZ shop. Sylvie has really bad posture and moves very slowly, exactly like one of the patients in the neighbourhood who is on the same drug. In former times, Sylvie used to go to the patients' club. Her mother was also a patient in Geel. So, mother and daughter went out together; the mother was always in charge.

Sylvie has no friends, neither men nor women. She always sits in a corner by herself. "It is impossible to know how or what she feels!", her foster father states. Some days, she is very stubborn. Some days she also eats in a very noisy and quite disgusting manner. When her foster parents reprimand her, and warn her that she will not be allowed to go out on Saturday if she does not stop, she does behave properly for a while, but pretty soon it all starts again. She endlessly repeats: "I am allowed to go out on Saturday, aren't I?"

An OPZ bus brings Sylvie home every afternoon. Her foster parents who like to cycle a lot have to be back home by the time she returns, as Sylvie does not know how to use keys and cannot enter the house. At dinner, Sylvie sometimes refuses to eat, as she is not hungry. On those occasions she has bought "delicious" French fries in downtown Geel. Time and time again her foster parents explain that she has to avoid fatty foods, but she happily ignores them. On Sundays Sylvie visits the club. Even though it is nearby, she cannot get there by herself.

Wherever she is, Sylvie always removes her watch and jewels when she uses the toilet. She has lost her belongings so many times now, it is no longer funny. Another one of her quirks is that she often steals a bar of soap in public places and puts it in her handbag while it is still wet. "I have plenty of money," is her only comment, "I have millions in my bank account!" She is not too bothered about losing her things. She has also lost her glasses several times. She is wearing double-focus glasses now, but does not know how to use them. She simply puts them on the tip of her nose.

Sylvie is not able to read. She simply flicks through magazines, making comments like: "What a pretty girl!" Sylvie feels that she equals (the young) Brigitte Bardot in beauty. She still remembers the days of Bardot. Her short-term memory is fading. Sylvie may be carrying something to the kitchen and suddenly forget what she is doing. She is not able to follow stories on television either, with the possible exception of a kid's movie.

Sylvie sometimes faces down her foster mother, and takes on a menacing posture. Her foster father has more impact on her. Sylvie is 53, but has never learned how to clean the house. She would clean herself into a corner. She has a bath every week, but does not rinse off the soap, leaving lots of foam in her ears. Repeatedly, Sylvie has tried to buy clothes without having obtained permission from her legal guardian. At other times she has refused to buy the clothes she desperately needs, arguing that she has more than enough clothes in her closet.

By Santa Claus and Christmas tension always runs high and Sylvie gets aggressive. Life would really be a nightmare without medication. Sylvie would not make it through the "happy season" without it. When she is nervous, Sylvie may go to the hair dresser's two or three times a day and may wear three sets of clothes, one on top of the other. Her parents had to bring her back to the Hospital one year because life had become impossible. There were times also when Sylvie did not dare cross the street. If forced to do so, she crawled to the other side on hands and knees, or she stopped in the middle of the street screaming for help.

The foster parents fear that foster care might be discontinued. Young people are afraid to commit, in their opinion. If the authorities want foster care to continue, they will have to raise the allowance. The present conditions are not attractive. For example, foster families do not receive any money for those days their patients spend at the Hospital, when their guests are on vacation, or when awaiting a new patient. Yet they feel it is likely that quite a few children will take over their parents' patient(s). One of their own daughters, who happened to be there during our discussion, admitted she will not become a foster mother, although she has very fond memories of the patients that lived with her family.

Sylvie comes back from work just as we are ready to leave. "They have beaten me up again!", she cries. "Impossible!", her foster father replies, "they would not dare beat up an attractive girl like you!" It shows that Sylvie is really very sick, as both foster parents have repeatedly stated. "But this is no reason to send her back," they continue, "she is not a thing but a human being."

2005

As I revisit the family in 2005, Sylvie hasn't changed much. She still shows compulsive behaviour. Lately she has started to frequently go to the toilet; all she does there is rinse the toilet over and over again which leads to an enormous waste of water. She turns the entire bathroom into a swimming pool. No improvement on that front. Keeping Sylvie home all day still is no option as she continuously interferes with everything. What has improved considerably is her panic attacks on the street. She can now cross the street without too much ado. Her medication has been adjusted and that seems to have been helpful. This makes her foster parents think it would be a good idea if the OPZ psychiatrists regularly stopped by at people's homes to closely follow up on their patients, especially the ones who are on heavy medication, and assess them in their home situation. At present, foster parents can only communicate directly with the district nurses and the latter are no experts in the area of medication. They certainly are not in a position to stop or alter the treatment.

It is still the foster father who paints Sylvie's nails and who helps her put on her necklace at the weekend. Just like five years ago, the foster parents confirm that they enjoy having Sylvie around and they would never send her away. The foster parents regret the OPZ hasn't managed to raise the allowances.

Comment

Living together with Sylvie would not be possible without the assistance from the OPZ. Both her job during the day and her medication are indispensable. The urgent need for medical supervision is demonstrated here. The OPZ staff and the foster family clearly complement each other. Caring for Sylvie is a joint effort. Quite a few people could not stay in a family if that sort of assistance was not on offer.

13) An incredibly difficult boarder, a member of the family all the same

2000

A huge house surrounded by barns, a yard and fields. The parents are living in one part of the house, their married son in the other. Louis (68) and his wife Anna (66) had been farming all their life when they retired seven years ago. They both grew up with boarders. The foster father's side of the family has a long history of foster care; his parents and both sets of grandparents used to host patients in their time. This is not the case for Anna's family, at least not to this extent. Louis and Anna both stem from farming families. During one of the interviews Louis volunteered the information that his parents had hosted an "angry" patient for 24 years. The latter couldn't and wouldn't tolerate another guest anywhere near him. His parents had tried as many as 12 different patients but to no avail. In January 2006 Anna and Louis will have been foster parents for 50 years.

Marcel (60), their present guest, arrived in their home 34 years ago. He is short and frail. The minute we entered the room for the interview, he walked out to buy bread at the village centre. Marcel runs simple errands, his most important purchase being cigarettes. Marcel has difficulty communicating. It is hard to picture him without a smile on his face. Marcel patronizes the OPZ club. He used to spend his vacation in Spain. This year, however, he will go to the Belgian coast, a destination for patients who require more care.

Marcel watched all the children grow up. Louis and Anna have five children: four daughters and a son. Next Sunday major celebrations take place in Geel and Marcel will accompany the family downtown. He is fond of the children and grandchildren. He would never ever tolerate a second patient in the house. The family hasn't even considered it. Both parents stress that Marcel is a very difficult person to live with, although some of their neighbours consider him a nice fellow. "Most foster families would send him back to the hospital 'in a flash'!", they say. Marcel has a short temper and regularly explodes. Even a few minor comments about the work he is expected to do can be fatal. Marcel cannot deal with getting orders and is extremely dominant. At least, that is how his foster parents see it. "We have been too easy on him!", they muse. They feel they are no longer in control. When Marcel gets infuriated, he turns white like a sheet and stops listening. He loses control and "screams his head off". To make matters worse, he used to live in a permanent state of war with his former district nurse. Marcel had been living with another family before coming here. These people cannot understand how the present family has put up with his behaviour all this time.

Marcel has the intelligence of a five-year-old. Once he starts working in the morning, he does not pause. His parents have to call him to a halt in the evening. "He is emotionally disturbed," is the diagnosis of one of the daughters who is a nurse. Marcel spent his youth in an orphanage in Wallonia. Louis and Anna assume that he had to fight to survive there. When he reminisces about the nuns in the orphanage, it invariably triggers an outburst. Marcel cannot read nor write, cannot read the clock and cannot deal with money. On Sundays, he gets approximately $35 of pocket money and some money for a drink at the club. His parents break down the money in small notes, so that the damage is limited when he gets cheated.

Difficult as it may have been (and still is), Marcel is there to stay. Louis and Anna still wonder why they stuck it out. "If it wasn't for us, where could he turn? Who would take him in?", is how they justify it. "Besides," they continue, "he has got a couple of things going for him as well: he does not steal and he is a child of the house. The children and grandchildren absolutely adore him." And it needs to be said, Marcel has always been very kind to their kids. And whenever grandchildren pop in, he is very friendly and warm. He shows off the new gadgets he has bought. Marcel has an impressive number of alarm clocks in his room and keeps adding to his collection. His alarms go off at various times, and he plays his music throughout the evening. "We would miss him dearly! We couldn't live with the idea that he is forced to stay with a family he is not happy with," Anna explains.

The foster parents were not informed by the OPZ that Marcel had a particularly difficult character. If they had known, they might not have taken him in. From time to time they wonder if it all makes sense. As a couple, they have never had any privacy. For years, Marcel was not the only guest. One of the grandfathers and an uncle were part of their household too.

"Marcel may look very sweet, but he is one of the worst 'gangsters' in Geel. There is a lot of anger in him, and he might use a knife or a fork as a weapon, one has to be very careful around him," the mother points out. One day, while sitting at the dinner table, he refused to eat, and made a move to leave. Louis made him sit down again. Marcel lashed out and broke a window. At occasions like that Marcel stamps his feet and bites. Over the past few years, he has calmed down somewhat. "We have been too permissive!", his parents comment. He once went mad when one of the daughters checked her make-up in the mirror while he was shaving.

In wintertime, the foster parents often go for a ride, just the two of them. Marcel loves to have the house all to himself. On these occasions, he makes coffee and watches television. He feels in charge then. Nobody is allowed in. Marcel is not fond of TV. He rarely watches, and does not understand. But if someone switches to another programme, he gets angry, and protests in a loud voice. Marcel walks around all the time in the sheds and the garden; he cannot sit still. He sometimes buys the same tape over and over again, and cannot withstand alarms and watches. On weekdays he wears two watches, one on his left and one on his right arm. He also buys all sorts of gadgets, and keeps swapping stuff with other patients.

The foster mother considers it her duty to look after her guest. If you take someone in, you have to be kind to him. Once in a while Anna complains to her children: "We have never had any time to ourselves, as a normal couple! You do not know what this means!"

Anna suggests that some foster parents might not take their job as a foster parent seriously and might even neglect their patient, but things have certainly improved. The "section guards" of yore sometimes turned a blind eye. In the days of the "hams" (so-called gifts, donated by the farmers), some guards were corrupt. "One of these guards might expect you to bring fresh milk to his house, daily. Some 40 years ago there used to be quite a number of bad boarding places," Anna remarks. Her husband agrees.

Louis and Anna travelled only once, in 1983. They visited Lourdes. They had won the trip and their children had insisted they go. The very day they returned, however, the uncle who had been living with them for years died.

Marcel is smart in his own fashion. When he feels like an outing, he "forgets" to buy his cigarettes as he fetches a loaf of bread. That way he can go out again. His bicycle is in tiptop shape. One day when he was shining his bicycle, the son of the house walked by and joked: "Why clean your bike? Just buy a new one!" A bit later, Marcel came home with a brand-new bicycle.

Marcel gets lost easily. Although he is familiar with his own neighbourhood, he is not able to make shortcuts. He always goes to the centre of the hamlet first, and then makes his way back. He tends to make a considerable detour. Marcel has his own shower and toilet upstairs. He is not allowed to use the family bathroom, as he usually takes more than half an hour to get ready.

On Sundays, the foster parents leave by themselves. They drive to a dancehall and stay there from 2 p.m. to 5 p.m. Marcel knows where to find the house-key should he be the first to return. On weekdays, the family sometimes drives to the local pilgrimage resort of Scherpenheuvel to attend mass and have lunch, just one of their favourite places to go.

"We have worked very hard our whole life. The positive side is that we simply lacked the time to get depressed!", the foster parents reflect. If one of the foster parents died, the other would try to keep Marcel. It might not be easy for Louis who is not exactly an expert cook. Anna is confident she could manage on her own.

Marcel regularly drops in at the children's homes. He gets a lot of clothes from them that are no longer trendy. He also buys clothes by himself, but often gets it wrong. He recently bought boots size 43, while his size is 38. When he makes a mistake like that, Marcel does not appreciate people commenting. He will wear his oversized boots, not an easy task.

Both foster parents think that it will be difficult to keep foster care alive in Geel. "There is too much luxury, too much money around. Besides it is increasingly difficult to host somebody for a mere 15 Euro ($20) a day, all included." Their own children won't commit either. Their son has married a woman from another town, and she is not used to living with guests. Moreover, the foster mother does not wish her children to take over Marcel, because he is a troublesome person.

2005

When I visit the family in 2005, they are living in a brand-new house built a bit further down the road. Their son and his family have taken over the farm. Marcel hasn't changed a bit; both his appearance and demeanour are the same. He still gets uncontrollable anger attacks. Sometimes they are so bad his foster parents truly despair. When the foster parents observed that Marcel's outbursts got worse and more frequent due to new medication, they were so desperate they stopped the treatment out of their own accord. They informed the OPZ team later. Anna and Louis feel that psychiatrists should personally follow up on medication prescribed, and this in the patient's home, so as to allow immediate interaction between the doctor and the foster parents. Long time ago, Dr Liekens, head of the Hospital in those days, used to regularly drop in to see how things were. The older foster parents reminisce about the old days and show their appreciation for this type of intervention, though they admit Dr Liekens was a bit of a weirdo too.

These days there is an extra complicating factor in Marcel's life: Marcel has got a girlfriend. Vera is her name. Vera and Marcel stir each other up in their revolt against their foster parents. At the annual barbecue, Marcel refused to go home with Anna and Louis. He wanted to stay with Vera. Vera doesn't visit with Marcel's family. Anna and Louis would not allow that anyway. A while ago, tension ran so high that Marcel, for the very first time, ran away from home to seek "refuge" in the OPZ. This incident has clearly made an impression on the foster parents. Just like five years ago, they suggest it is all their fault. They haven't been strict enough with their guest. With hindsight, they wouldn't have embarked on this journey with Marcel.

Even so, in spite of the ongoing tension and difficulties, Anna and Louis do not intend to send their guest away. They will carry on, no matter how difficult it is. They expressed this very same opinion five years ago. Even if they weren't paid at all, they would still look after him. This doesn't mean, however, that they think the pay is sufficient. They do feel it is on the low side. Another matter they regret is that the natural families only surface once the patients are dead and buried. They never have any time for the patient, and only show up at the funeral for the inheritance.

Comment

Life with patients certainly takes its toll. Sometimes their behaviour is so appalling, one can hardly imagine how families cope. But even these "difficult" patients are eventually embraced with love and affection, and as years go by, they truly become part of the family. In the above case, Marcel's only redeeming feature is that he has always been really sweet to the children and grandchildren. That surely was to his advantage.

14) Sisters forever

2000

A middle-class house, well maintained, close to the centre of Geel. The foster mother, Irène, 60, has decades of professional experience as a psychiatric nurse in several mental hospitals, including the one in Geel. For long years she combined a part-time job with fostering. Irène knows the life in mental institutions inside out. Irène grew up with guests in her family. Irène's mother, who is 90 now, hosted a White-Russian patient for more than 50 years. This patient, Boris, had fled his country when still a young man, and ended up in Geel via Ireland. He fluently spoke French, and the members of the foster family picked up quite a lot of French through Boris. The latter suffered from epilepsy, but was an extremely effective domestic help. His foster mother was so pleased with his services that she paid him a salary.

Irène's guest, Louise, a lady in her early 70s, entered the family more than 30 years ago. Louise can read and write four languages and worked as an administrator in a university laboratory for advanced research before coming to Geel. "I am less well versed in German," she apologized, "as the Germans executed my father." When in the evening the lights of a neighbouring school illuminate the sky, Louise stands near the window "in order to pick up special messages". According to her foster mother, Louise has a very strong intuition and manages to quickly and accurately assess a person.

Although her parents were rather wealthy—her father was a big spender—Louise's youth wasn't a bed of roses. Her parents continually fought for years. Louise's foster mother describes her as a beautiful young woman, and photographs confirm this. Louise married a university graduate but the marriage didn't last. It broke her, and her life went downhill from there. She went from one mental institution to another. Over and over again, Louise made plans to leave institutional mental care behind and pick up the pieces, but her psychiatrists never let her go. The OPZ medical director refused to set her free too. Louise does not like what she sees in Geel. "It is incredible, the characters you meet in Geel!", she says. "I do not feel at home with these people." This is the reason why Louise refuses to go out in town on weekends. She does not visit the patients' club either. She used to have a few female friends at one point, but one of them turned out to be a kleptomaniac. Her thorough dislike for psychiatric hospitals notwithstanding, Louise agrees to spend some time at the Hospital when her foster parents go on their annual skiing holiday. Louise joins her foster parents when they are on a holiday at the Belgian coast. Previously, she used to spend her own holidays with the OPZ in Spain, or on the Baleares.

Louise likes to discuss the lives of princes and wealthy lawyers, and allegedly knew a member of the House of Habsburg at Louvain University. Louise reads a lot, whatever she can lay her hands on. *Time Magazine* is one of her favourites. She refuses to read newspapers, however: "They only talk about murders!" Louise has a vivid imagination too. She saw both the son and the daughter of her foster family grow up. Her relationship with the children has always been excellent. When Irène was still working as a nurse, Louise locked up the house after the children had left for school. She has always been very careful and reliable. The now-married son jokes a lot with Louise when he is visiting, much to her pleasure.

When she was younger, Louise held an important, administrative position in the Geel OPZ Hospital. Now that she is in her 70s, her job is less complex. After coming home in the late afternoon, she talks to her foster mother for hours on end. The foster mother describes these chats as meaningful exchanges between friends. They discuss anything. The foster father does not join them in their chats. Louise used to keep a secret diary, but she burnt it before undergoing surgery, "because," she says, "it contained passages that might offend some members of my foster family."

Louise loves to be waited on and never feels like a pauper. She invariably shows gratitude, and only occasionally asks if she can be of any help. She also gives small presents to her foster parents' grandchildren. She regrets not having any of her own. Louise will not tolerate a second patient in the house. When her foster parents took in a second guest on probation, Louise forced them to take her back to the Hospital.

Over the years, there have been quite a number of, mostly unannounced, visits from two of Louise's sisters. One of them died recently. The other sister lives in a wealthy suburb, somewhere in the US. Both sisters were experiencing psychiatric problems at the time of their visits. These visits caused a lot of problems in the foster family, and were detrimental to Louise's mental health. The OPZ psychiatrists strongly discouraged further meetings with the patient's relatives.

2005

As I revisited the foster family in 2005, Louise had been dead for two years. The foster family had grieved for a long time, and then "all hell broke lose," according to the foster mother. After Louise's death the OPZ proposed a number of candidates, none of whom were a success.

The first lady that stayed with them was Margo. She was about 42 years old but looked more like a very pretty 25-year-old. When they first met, Margo immediately stated "she wanted to go and live with this attractive lady." The first few weeks everything ran like clockwork. Irène's knowledge of Margo was extremely limited: the district nurse had merely said that Margo was a special case, nothing more. The rest of Margo's life story was disclosed bit by bit, as time went by.

Pretty soon Margo started to do her own thing irrespective of what the family thought was appropriate. She ate with the family, but that was about the extent of her commitment. Irène let her have her way because she figured Margo knew what she was doing. However, Margo was at home less and less and after a while Irène found out she was involved with a man. Margo wanted to sleep at his place. The foster father could not deal with that, and discussed it with the OPZ. It was decided not to go down this path, and Margo agreed.

But soon she went from one to two boyfriends, and then to many. Some would stop at the house in expensive cars. The family increasingly received phone calls from strangers and eventually received threatening stuff in the mail box, which had the name of the underworld written all over it. Margo had obviously become involved with prostitution. The family even had the impression their house was being watched by members of a criminal gang, and that was the last straw. Margo left the very same day. Irène was extremely upset with the OPZ for not having discussed Margo's past with her.

The next boarder was Maria (65). She stayed only one week. She used to be a teacher. She was so dominating, the foster parents almost immediately lost heart. She told them which rooms had to be heated, how Irène should run her household and even commented on Louis's slippers. As soon as the foster parents reacted, she announced that it was their job to support her in her search for freedom and a full life, and not to order her about. This ended the relationship. Maria had been in another foster family prior to this one, a family with young children. This family too had sent Maria back to the OPZ.

Irène, an experienced nurse herself, wonders whether patients like the ones mentioned above are suitable for foster care. She is not convinced. A dominant patient, keen on independence, is not easy to accommodate in a family. A family should be able to exercise some authority over the guests. The latter may seem capable at first glance to lead their lives without too much assistance from the family, but very often their shortcomings are merely masked by medication. Only after a while does it become clear which skills these people lack and which behavioural problems they have got. According to Irène, people with a very long experience, because they have grown up with patients of all walks of life, see through this apparent self-sufficiency sooner rather than later.

Comment

This foster mother's reflections about recent patients closely resemble those made in cases 6 and 8.

15) Problematic

2000

Marina (31) and René (34), are among the youngest foster parents. They are self-employed and run a modern agro-business. They have two children, four and six years old. The foster mother also teaches in Geel. John (21), their guest, arrived 18 months ago.

The foster father is from another town where "the loonies" are a distant notion. René had no prior experience with mental patients, unlike his wife. Marina grew up with boarders. Her grandparents on both sides of the family hosted patients, and her mother still has a guest. Both Marina's parents and grandparents encouraged her to go ahead and commit, as she had an empty spare room in her spacious new home.

The first guest they took in was Norbert. Norbert had spent some 30 years in a closed institution before coming to Geel, and had tried to integrate in several other families. His relationship with the children of the family was first-rate. He was a clever man, able to read and write. From time to time he started talking about his past. His depressed mother had committed suicide while he was supposed to look after her. His father and other relatives had never forgiven him. They had stopped speaking to him altogether. Holidays like Christmas, New Year and Easter, when other patients go home, were particularly hard for Norbert.

Norbert avoided places like the patients' club. He wanted to be alone: "I am different, not like them!", he used to say. He wanted to live by himself in sheltered accommodation. At given times he envied the young foster family he lived with and got severely depressed. He let his head hang down and rocked on his chair. The family had struck a deal with Norbert and the district nurse, that he would no longer bring up his problems in the presence of the children. From time to time, Norbert broached nasty questions, also about religion, definitely not suitable for young ears. When in a depressive mood, Norbert used to smoke three packets of cigarettes a day. He also had to take heavy medication.

Norbert helped his foster father with some minor tasks in the morning, then had breakfast and went off to the workshop. Norbert had, unlike the present guest, an outspoken feeling of belonging. When the children were in bed at night, he discussed his problems with his foster parents. At a given time, Marina and René felt that suicide was constantly on his mind. They feared that an "accident" might occur. They were terrified that their children might run into Norbert's body. That was the reason why they sent Norbert back to the OPZ.

John, their present guest, had also lived with several families before coming to Marina and René's place. It hadn't worked out at all. John is very different from Norbert. John keeps to himself. He sometimes says a few words to his foster mother, but mostly he is silent. He doesn't go anyway near the children. John listens to all possible kinds of music. He is allowed to play his music as loud as he pleases in the barn only, not in the house. John made a deal with his foster parents, that he would have one piercing and wear one ring only. Later John wanted more piercings and a conflict erupted. The district nurse took the parents' side.

It looks as if John has stopped drinking alcohol. He used to be a heavy drinker before. There is a stipulation in the contract John signed, that if he is drinks again, he will take a drug to remedy his drinking problem. As this drug really puts him off, John has stayed away from alcohol. He has gotten drunk only twice since he arrived in his present family. Sundays, John leaves by bicycle. He never informs his foster parents about what he is doing, but they know that he has fallen in love with a young lady. She is not a patient.

When asked a question, John remains silent and stares at the floor. He reacts in the same way when he faces the male district nurse. It is striking that he always adopts the same attitude when confronted with men. John starts to tremble when his foster father raises his voice. "His father possibly beat him up," Marina thinks. John's mother had five children from three different fathers. John's last stepfather had a son of his own, and did not want John anywhere near him for fear that John's "madness" was contagious.

Until recently, John stayed in touch with his sister. She asked him to be the godfather of her child. His social worker gave him money to buy a present for the baby, but John spent it all on other things and did not even bother to attend the christening. As a result, he is no longer welcome at his sister's place. John is not sociable. He does not care about other people, unless it suits him. The last few weeks his behaviour has gone downhill. Marina and René do not get any affection in return. Their former patient used to be grateful; not so with John. Talking to John is only periodically possible. John may stay out of reach for weeks.

Before coming to Geel, John was placed in a home after being caught with drugs. He arrived in his present foster family 18 months ago. René and Marina both feel there has been little improvement. Even the smallest task he is asked to perform in the morning is too much for him. Again and again, he has to be corrected. "Like a child!", his foster parents comment. After making his minor contribution, mostly in a sloppy fashion, John leaves for the OPZ workshop at a time he deems fit. Occasionally, Marina sees him hanging around in the shopping area downtown Geel, two hours after leaving the house.

John has his own TV in his room. In order to prevent John watching TV all night, René installed a timer, but John doctored the mechanism over and over again. An intervention by the district nurse did not help. Eventually, the TV was removed from John's room for two weeks. John did not protest at all and never asked a question. John never asks for anything. He has a major problem with communication. Some days, he approaches his foster parents up to ten times with the clear intention to start talking, but he never does. Marina is concerned about the children. Whenever the children are out of sight while John is in the house, she checks.

John goes on vacation to Spain. He also practises various sports like table tennis and walking, and went on a "survival" trip to the Ardennes. On given occasions John takes a selection of his CDs to the OPZ where he performs as an amateur-DJ, as he used to do at the annual barbecues for the foster parents and their boarders. John can read. He also writes, but in capital letters only. He borrows books from the public library like his foster parents, but does not read them.

Some of their friends wonder why Marina and René took in a patient. They do not understand.

2005

In 2005 Marina and René no longer host any guests.

16) Quite a challenge

2000

Lea (40) is one of the younger foster mothers. Louise (62), her guest, is of Black-African origin. At the time of our visit Lea's relationship with Louise was problematic. Louise ended up going to the Hospital for the week, because life had become impossible. Lea is delighted that she gets a chance to talk. (In our discussion below a number of confidential issues are left out.)

Both foster parents grew up between guests. The foster mother's parents and one of her sisters live nearby. Louise arrived in this household a year ago, but she hasn't "bonded" so far. Before, Louise stayed with one of Lea's grandmothers who was very old and ill. Louise looked after her, cleaning the house, cooking, and monitoring her medication. Louise wasn't up to running a household all by herself. Everything got increasingly grubby. According to Lea, the OPZ made a mistake not stepping in at an earlier stage. Fortunately, Lea's grandmother was quite a figure who kept Louise under control. Lea says that she herself is too soft: no match for Louise. Louise is incredibly fond of shopping and tells all kinds of nonsense to the people she meets, like: "Do you want to win 90 million?" She also spreads the rumour that her foster father is a womanizer, that he is always abroad, and that her foster mother flirts with other men. Louise is a terrible gossip.

The son of the house, who is 12, does not like all the fuss. Louise does not stop talking when she watches TV. She cherishes soaps and comes downstairs to watch television. She won't miss any of it. She has an immense clock in her room. The television-set in the living room is hers. She seems a capable person and is well aware of what is going on. She speaks French fluently.

Lea is alone with Louise all day long. Her husband leaves very early in the morning and returns late at night. Louise stresses her out. She is sick and tired of Louise babbling on and on. Lately, the situation has gotten out of hand and Louise was taken to hospital. The foster mother intends to give it a new chance at the end of the week, but if things don't improve she will quit. The district nurse told her that there are other patients looking for a foster family and that she would be eligible.

Nobody in the neighbourhood truly knows Louise yet. Even the parish priest called to have a word with Lea about Louise's feats. Louise apparently randomly rings people's doorbells with the request to use their phone to call her brothers. Her three brothers all live at various mental institutions. Louise recounts that she was battered by her father, that she was brought to a convent where she fell ill, and that the nuns sent her to Geel. Every year, these nuns pick her up in Geel and bring her to one of her brothers who lives in Brussels. They receive about 7,000 francs (about 155 dollar) from Louise's account in return for this trip. The foster parents also drive Louise to her brother once a year. They do it for free.

Recently, Louise entered Lea's parents' house and started scolding, just like that, out of the blue. She hasn't apologized yet. The past few weeks, Louise has been extremely stubborn. She declines orders, hides dirty linen and handkerchiefs all over the house, no longer cleans her teeth, etc. Even though she has only one front tooth left, she refuses to see the dentist. She extracts her own teeth. She also declines to work at the OPZ, although a day-job at the OPZ might be a huge relief to the family.

Louise is afraid of the district nurse, but once he has left she calls him a devil. "He lives off our misery! He just comes here to bully us!", she shouts. In Louise's eyes, everybody is unkind to her. "They are all evil in Geel," she says. People should allow her to phone her brothers, "because it is God's will". She tells her foster mother that she likes the house, but not the people who live in it. "My brothers are the only people I love."

When Louise arrived at her present post, she was in bad shape. She had been lacking proper food and care for a long time. The patient has put on considerable weight since her arrival. Louise is very "Catholic". She fears she will die soon. Louise is scared of dying. She is counting the years. "I am 62 already!", she repeats over and over again. However, when the OPZ ambulance took her to the Hospital last week, she screamed that she wanted to die.

The son of the family is relieved that Louise is not there for a while. Her behaviour is particularly embarrassing when his friends visit. Louise helps with the household but does not clean properly. She does the dishes indifferently and sloppily, at least to the taste of her foster mother who confesses she is quite demanding. This year, the foster mother will spend a week at the seaside and her mother will take care of Louise. Louise does not want to go away. She refuses to get into a car, lest she dies in an accident.

Louise rocks in her chair. "I am really stressed out by Louise's behaviour," the foster mother says, "I do not now how to handle her." Louise also refuses to go to the wellness centre. She used to visit the club and had a much younger boyfriend. These days, Louise professes that she does not want to have anything to do with men anymore. She pities her foster mother for her married state. "Giving birth to children is very painful," she says.

Louise goes to church on Sundays. She knows the value of coins and bills. She tends to split people. She also reads and writes, and keeps a pile of letters in her room, mostly sent by her brothers. She also keeps all sorts of other papers. The OPZ doctor recently called to ask Lea if the family was prepared to take in a second patient, as she had rooms available. Louise erupted in fury. "I do not want a loony in this house! I am not a loony!", was her reaction.

2006

As we visit in 2006, the foster mother volunteers Louise's behaviour hasn't improved much over the past few years, the opposite holds in fact. Louise (68) was admitted to the OPZ at least twice due to bad behaviour. She had severely threatened her foster mother, she had been aggressive and had expressed extreme anger and rage. Louise is on heavy tranquilizers now.

In the past, Louise used to surprise members of the family with a small gift for their birthday. Not anymore. She only thinks of herself. To make matters worse, she started buying cakes for herself and charged them to her foster mother's expense account. She secretly devoured them when walking home from the bakery. The foster mother only found out when the bakery bill spun out of control, and neighbours reported that they had seen Louise eating in the street. Louise gets up early in the morning and has eaten quite a bit by the time the others appear at the breakfast table.

The foster mother doubts whether she will be able to keep Louise in the long term. So far, her husband and the district nurse have been able to persuade her to go on. As opposed to what she used to do, Louise does not join the family to watch television at night. Around 7.30 p.m. she goes to her own bedroom. There is no way around it, this is what she wants. "She is a very secretive person," the foster mother states.

Louise has two boyfriends, both are about 20 years her junior. Louise goes to the OPZ pub with her mates every Sunday. She is picked up by the bus. On Wednesdays Louise goes to the OPZ workshop where she mainly works on mailings. The foster mother now has a half-time position; she works from 6 p.m. until 10 p.m. during the week. Death terrifies Louise. She keeps asking people around her whether they are afraid to die too. She used to attend mass every single Sunday. Recently, she asked the priest to relieve her of her Sunday duty, though, because of her advanced age. He did. The family's son, who has recently turned 18, no longer objects to Louise living there.

Halfway through our conversation, Louise joins us. During the first phase of our interview we do not recognize any signs of serious mental problems. Louise feels she doesn't see her brothers, all of whom are younger, often enough. Louise recounts that she spent four years in a convent, but that she couldn't manage and became ill. That's how she ended up in Geel. Her former fellow-sisters still keep in touch with her. Louise explains that she doesn't have two but three mates, one of whom is merely a friend to talk to. The other two are more than just friends; they are boyfriends. She feels it is normal to have more than one boyfriend. According to her foster mother, she is absolutely crazy about one of her partners. Louise, as it happens, seems rather keen on men in general.

Comment
From what I gather, Louise won't be sent back in a hurry to the OPZ. She did take care of her current foster mother's sick grandmother, and that gave her a certain status in the family. But the situation remains precarious. One of the main and crucial ingredients lacking in this foster home is a mutual and cordial family relationship. The cement is missing somehow.

17) Foster parents, new to the system

2000
A very spacious, comfortable restored farm in rural Geel. Lea and Paul are both 59. Their adult children live elsewhere. Both foster parents belong to the upper middle-class. They originate from another region of Flanders and have spent long years abroad, in various countries of the world. The foster father is a university graduate and has an important job in a major international company. Lea and Paul felt that their house was too big and empty after their children had left. They first considered taking in students from a nearby college, but

dropped the idea lest students might turn out too noisy. Eventually, Lea got acquainted with foster care through local connections, and they took in an OPZ patient.

Their guest, Felix, is 65. He works at a workshop on weekdays. Felix arrived in the family three years ago. His foster parents are under the distinct impression that he has never been fond of hard work. That is probably why Felix's father, who was an entrepreneur, sent him away. After leaving his father's business, Felix became a labourer in one of Flanders' major sea ports, and eventually took a job as a bus driver. He did not like being employed by private firms because, according to his own standards, they worked him too hard. Felix tends to be depressed. He got married, then divorced, and married a second time. His second wife died from cancer. Felix has four children. They never visit. Before he came to Geel, a few years ago, Felix drove his own car and managed his own money. It was quite a blow to him when he had to give up all that. Felix had been living in sheltered accommodation for seven years and managed to set aside an important sum of money. He is extremely obsessed with his "money". He keeps his money in his bank account, and feels quite wealthy, not to say filthy rich. Felix seems to save this money for his children, for times to come, and gets in trouble again and again because of his attitude towards money. He once complained that his money was stolen from his room, an insinuation that was quite embarrassing to his foster parents and strained their relationship.

Felix doesn't talk to anybody. His foster mother tried to initiate communication repeatedly, without success. The foster parents offered Felix his own living-room, shower and TV, so that everybody in the house could keep his own privacy. Felix agreed. Felix does not object to working at the OPZ, but when he comes home in the evening, he says he is too tired to help out in the garden.

Sundays, Felix leaves on his bike and has a pub-lunch in the neighbourhood, preferably by himself. He does not visit the patients' club. He feels that the guys over there are too simple, and considers himself superior. Felix also reads and watches television. When the foster parents leave on a holiday abroad, Felix moves into the Hospital. He refuses to travel himself, estimating that he has seen enough of the world. After all, he has been to Egypt, Italy and Spain. He also refuses to go on vacation with the other patients. "They do not even listen to the explanations provided by the guide," he comments. All the same, Felix does join the party for day-trips and likes to go to the OPZ bathhouse. Lea and Paul feel that money should not be the main motive to take in patients, but they are convinced that if the amount were raised, it would be easier to attract young families.

2005

Lea and Paul moved away some time prior to my visit. They no longer live in Geel.

For some years now the OPZ has been recruiting foster families in the villages surrounding Geel, so as to increase the potential number of candidates. These attempts have proved fairly successful. In most cases one of the members of the family originates from Geel or has first-hand experience. These families "extra muros" are given the same level of services; the OPZ is available day and night.
In 2006 I visited two families.

18) A new foster mother in the periphery of Geel

Hélène and her foster daughter live in a sort of garage that has been turned into a temporary house. Hélène is about 45 years old and so is her guest, Gina. When I visit, her aged mother from Geel is sitting at the table. Gina is not there as she has gone to work in Geel. She travels by bus to and from work. Occasionally, she falls asleep and misses her bus stop. Every time she manages to find her way back. She invariably blames it on the bus driver "who got lost".

Gina is very fickle as far as her mood is concerned. She may be emotional for weeks on end. She wants to be hugged all the time which her foster mother carefully declines. Other times, she is distant and difficult. She says nasty things about her foster mother to the neighbours. "I have burst out into tears again and again," Hélène admits. One of her friends confronted her about this, and said that she had no idea what she had gotten herself into.

Gina has threatened several times that she would take a kitchen knife and harm herself, or that she would burn her arm with cigarettes. She has never directed her threats to Hélène. The latter alleges that she couldn't have coped during this first phase without the district nurse's efficient support. The nurse pulled her through, because he persuaded her she should not blame herself for not coping all that well. Gina displays difficult behaviour and suffers from mood swings. That doesn't imply that the foster mother's approach is inadequate.

Gina alleges she has been pregnant twice, but she miscarried. She was married, that much we do know. Hélène refers to her foster daughter as a patient of the new generation, not the placid, well-meaning type of yore, but a person more difficult to deal with.

Every Sunday Gina goes to Geel. She has a boyfriend called Guido. According to Hélène, Guido is an amiable enough man. He sent her flowers once. Guido never visits, even though Hélène wouldn't mind at all if he did.

Occasionally, Gina drops in on the neighbours. People do not seem to appreciate this all that much apart from an elderly lady, who rather enjoyed the visits—at first that is. After a while she thought these visits too strenuous. This does not mean that her neighbours disapproved of Hélène's decision to take in a psychiatric patient. On the contrary, they showed their appreciation and even admired her for doing so. There were no negative reactions. Hélène is a family help who regularly works in Geel. That's how she got acquainted with the system and got the idea to foster herself.

During the matching process, Gina put forward one condition: she needed a family that would also host her two dogs. Since the foster mother is a proud dog-owner herself, this wasn't an issue. They have got their love for dogs in common.

19) A second family in Meerhout

This is a young family with two little girls, one is seven, the other eleven. The family home is a recently-built, pretty house. The foster father, Bruno, has a maintenance job in Geel. The foster mother, Vera, has a job as well. They used to own a big dog but it got killed by a car when the patient was walking it. They now own a German shepherd. Bruno originates from Geel and had patients in his own family. He grew up amongst them. Vera is from Meerhout, and as such not familiar with fostering psychiatric patients. Both their neighbours and friends reacted positively when they announced their intention to start fostering. Germaine, the patient in question, was welcomed in the neighbourhood.

As stated before, Karel and Vera both have a job, but on Fridays they are at home, and so is Germaine. On that day they all clean the house together, an arrangement that seems to work really well.

Germaine is in her 50s. Sitting in her chair, sort of shrunk to half her size, she doesn't look at me, not even when she speaks to me. She rocks her chair non-stop. She fell from one depression into the next, she says. Her father died at the age of 50, her mother was in her 80s. Following the death of her mother, Germaine started wandering. Prior to coming to Geel, she had been admitted to several hospitals. Germaine has to walk about a kilometre to take the bus to work. She has absolutely no problems coping on her own. Every weekend she takes the bus to Geel to go and have a coffee with her friend. She leaves about 9 a.m. and comes home around 5 p.m. When it is dark, she doesn't venture outside since she is afraid somebody might assault her.

Comment

The district nurses tell me that, as far as they know, there haven't been any negative reactions in the communities surrounding Geel following a placement of a psychiatric patient.
In principle, one honours and respects the family care system and its foster parents. Sometimes a neighbour might get irritated if a patient doesn't respect his/her privacy. This is different in Geel where people have grown more tolerant over the years; in our research at least, we haven't come across similar situations.

| Chapter V |
The Geel tradition

Relationship between the guest and his/her family

From the cases, some recurrent patterns and themes emerged, even though they were worded differently by interviewees. Together, they can be considered the foundations of the Geel psychiatric foster care system, a tradition that is handed down from one generation to the next.

Folk wisdom and science

Leading reference works like *DSM-IV* (1997) stipulate that diagnosing mental disorders is a complex matter. What persons with psychological problems say and manifest is often difficult to classify into clear-cut categories. Moreover, quite a number of individuals share a number of symptoms but differ substantially in other respects. This is exactly what Geelian foster parents stress when discussing the behaviour of their boarders: although all patients are mentally retarded and/or mentally ill, they are all unique. Most foster parents are quite experienced, as they have either lived with several patients in their own home, or have been in close contact with them for a substantial part of their life.

Even so, foster parents are not familiar with psychological of psychiatric categories, let alone classification systems. This was demonstrated in our research of 1971-75 and confirmed in our 1999-2000 fieldwork. Not a single foster parent in our sample had ever consulted a handbook of psychology or psychiatry, nor had one asked physicians or psychiatrists for "learned" explanations about the "illness" of one's patient. The average degree of formal education of the foster parents is quite basic, which partly explains this so-called lack of interest. The OPZ professionals, however, reinforce this attitude by limiting the information they provide to a strict minimum. Very little is told about the patient's origin, family history, track record and previous hospitalization(s). Until fairly recently, nothing was communicated at all. Even today, briefings by staff are kept to a minimum. This was and is a conscious decision. The main goal is to give patients a fresh start, unencumbered by the past. Both case managers and foster parents agree that it is wise not to explore the patient's personal history and not to ask too many questions. Nobody benefits from dragging up the past. The risk of surfacing memories and emotions that are very unsettling and hard to control is not worth taking. Evidently, over the years, bit by bit, elements of the patient's previous life will come to light but, by that time patients have, hopefully, settled and established a rapport with the family and its environment.

Folk classifications

This doesn't mean foster parents aren't interested in pragmatic issues. They are keen to find out how their new patient behaves, what s/he does well, where his/her interests lie, what impact his/her disabilities have on daily life and so on. Interestingly, foster parents have their own, rudimentary folk classifications. You have "good" patients and "difficult" ones. A good patient is an easygoing companion in daily life, does not disturb the family's routines, reciprocates love and bonds. S/he is loyal to the foster family, behaves as "one of them", and defends his/her relatives' reputation when necessary. Additionally, a good patient lends a helping hand in the household. S/he might take on chores like cooking, cleaning, babysitting or gardening. Alternatively, guests work in an OPZ workshop during the day. Usually, foster parents take into their stride occasional "accidents" in the domain of personal hygiene or instances of stubborn or even slightly deviant behavior. This is what one expects even from good patients. In case two or three patients live in the same foster home, foster parents praise themselves lucky when their guests get along fine. As patients tend to arrive one at a time, this is often the case. If a newcomer is not compatible with the other(s), more often than not s/he will move on to another household.

A "difficult" boarder, on the other hand—exceptionally referred to as "bad"—considerably complicates life. S/he obstructs, refuses to abide by the rules set by the family, and even challenges his/her case manager or "the Colony". A patient categorized as such easily lies, does not return affection, does not show attachment or gratitude, and might come across as "cold". A "difficult" patient frequently throws fits, neglects personal hygiene, refuses to wash, dominates or even menaces his/her foster parents. Remarkably, foster parents in charge of a "difficult" patient for considerable lengths of time or even for good, aren't necessarily stressed out. Joking relations and humour go a long way and turn out to be excellent coping strategies. Most foster parents do assume that their patients will mellow over the years. And indeed, their patience often pays off. But, of course, some patients degenerate instead.

It goes without saying that boarders are neither all-good, nor all-bad. There are many shades in between. No foster parent has ever devised an exact scale. Even so, norms seem to be quite standardized, and entirely subjective evaluations are very rare. Foster families do talk to one another, compare and comment. Some sort of subcultural standard of assessment has emerged. Of course, how one classifies a given patient also depends to some extent on one's own expectations and reference frame.

Social integration

Social integration is a first rule of thumb. Every single foster parent tries to integrate the guest in his family as best he can: "He is one of us"; "he is involved in everything"; "if you do not allow them to be a part of the family, better not to take on guys from the Colony"; "she is a family member"; "we do not talk about Leo as a patient, he is 'our Leo'." Inclusion must be applied to all aspects of daily life. Foster parents disapprove of any foster family that does not rigorously respect this rule of social integration.

Quality of food is a similarly important. It is absolutely unacceptable, that patients are forced to eat or sit by themselves, separated from the family; that boarders are served dishes of lower quality, or get different food. The opposite holds. Even in our times, when putting on weight is generally frowned upon, it is still a sure sign of good treatment in Geel. Weight gain in the first months in a foster family is solid evidence that all is well.

Inclusion also pertains to sleeping patterns. To send a patient to bed at an early hour is another form of exclusion that is not considered acceptable. A minority of foster parents defensively mentions that their patient usually goes to bed early on his/her own initiative. A few patients do go to bed as early as 6 p.m. or 7 p.m. They sort of follow a seasonal pattern:

They go to bed early in winter and at a later hour in summer. "But nobody is forced to do so," foster parents hasten to add. Of course, if a patient retires early, this allows for more privacy in the family. Nevertheless, it should never be contrived.

Watching television is another critical issue. These days, many patients have their own television in their bedroom. At our remark that quite a number of patients watch television in their bedroom, foster parents replied that this was no sign of exclusion. Patients are said to do so on their own initiative because they want to watch their own shows. Invariably, families add that their patients are more than welcome to join the family. Some families even consider it a duty to watch television together if not all the time, at least for a substantial part of the evening. In that case compromises are made and flexibility is expected. Foster parents may condemn themselves to enduring children's programmes, relentless soaps, game shows, or, at times of championships, football matches. In a couple of houses we spotted a television set in two adjoining rooms in the veranda, allowing the members of the household to sit together while watching different programmes. In another house, we noticed a television set in each of the two adjoining sitting rooms. The foster mother hastened to explain that this did not imply that the two male boarders had to sit apart in the evenings. Quite to the contrary, she stressed that her husband tended to join "the guys" while she sat by herself.

Sitting apart turns out to be quite a sensitive issue. During an interview, a foster mother confided she was not sure what to make of her fellow foster mother and good neighbour. While it is clear she considered the neighbour a nice person, her colleague's patient was used to sitting by herself in the barn. That obviously threw her off and made her feel uneasy. Case managers pay special attention to the issue of sitting apart or together. If a patient, for instance, repeatedly hesitates to enter the family room during their visit, they make a mental note of it. It might indicate that the guest has been conditioned not to enter the room and is kept apart.

During our research in the late nineties, we came across two cases in which the patient was not allowed to use the family toilet, but was forced to use the fields behind the house, and to bury his excrements with a spade. In one of the two cases this practice seemingly had gone on for 30 years. The patient had kept silent all this time because he feared that he would be transferred to another family that could even be worse. After the district nurse had carefully checked the facts, he "removed" the patient from the family home and admitted him to hospital. This is considered an absolute disgrace in the Geel community. The community implicitly has a rule of zero tolerance to that sort of behaviour. Minor infractions too come to light from time to time. In a particular family the case manager discovered that the patient had to use his own cutlery: his knife, fork and spoon were discretely marked.

In general, one can state that foster parents see it as their responsibility to include a patient in their life. They realize all too well, that a lasting relationship is not possible without this sort of commitment. But, it takes two to dance. Patients too must be aware of the value of inclusion. Some react badly to being approached. "She can go on, day after day, ignoring signs of affection, refusing love." More often than not this marks the end of a family's commitment to a patient. If there is no response whatsoever, the patient may be sent back to the OPZ, a measure every foster family can resort to any time. If the patient turns down inclusion, foster parents can apply for another patient as they aren't seen as having failed.

"Inclusion" and "exclusion", of course, are variable concepts, depending to some extent on context. Consider the following examples:

> *When a visitor enters the house where boarder Mon (75) lives, the patient is used to welcoming him/her with loud cries and repeated handshakes. Mon then continues to mumble loudly while standing very close to the visitor, even after the guest is seated. Usually, the foster mother asks Mon to take a seat in an adjoining room, so that normal, undisturbed conversation can take place. This measure is not considered a sign of exclusion, but simply a means to make cohabitation possible.*

> *As Joseph, another patient, compulsively "steals any money he can get his hands on", it is agreed that under no circumstances he is allowed to enter the bedroom of his foster parents where the valuables of the house are kept. The same may apply to patients who are drug addicts, and who search the house high and low for drugs of any kind, including their own medication which they might swallow in one hit, overdosing themselves.*

Generally speaking, participation in the life of the family is far-reaching. The overwhelming majority of foster parents we visited never go on vacation. Those who do, tend to take their patient with them, be it to the Belgian coast, to Italy or even to Portugal. They do this out of their own accord, certainly not out of necessity. If asked, the OPZ temporarily admits the patient to the Hospital while the foster family is on vacation, or arranges a stay with a "guest family", provided the patient agrees.

> *Marie-Louise (63) accompanies her much younger foster parents on their vacation to Italy for two weeks.*

> *Robert (52) regularly spends two weeks at the Belgian coast with his foster parents.*

> *Roger's official foster parents annually spend eight months in Portugal while Roger stays in Geel in the care of their son. Around New Year, the son's family and Roger drive all of 2,500 km to join the "official" foster parents in their bungalow in Portugal. They all spend a couple of weeks together. Roger boasts he has three rooms: a room in the house of his foster parents in Geel, one in their son's house, and yet another one in Portugal.*

It is absolute routine to invite patients to all kinds of celebrations: weddings, confirmation parties, anniversaries, etc. It has also become quite common for patients to throw a party and pay for it with their own money. They may celebrate their 50th or 60th birthday; their being in Geel for 30 years; the anniversary of their arrival in the foster family; an important birthday of one of their foster parents. In short, any reason will do to celebrate being part of a family and community. Occasionally, patients may also invite their "sweetheart", their boyfriend or girlfriend.

Minor, fairly low-key celebrations, like birthday parties, are common in almost all families. These practices are also widespread in the workshops. Some patients "specialize" in memorizing the birthdays of people dear to them, like the members of their foster family or their colleagues at their workplace. Again and again throughout our fieldwork, we were offered birthday cakes and cookies. All these celebrations are a means to, and an expression of integration. Birthday parties in particular stress social equality: everybody has a birthday, no special talents or merits are required. Presents, whether big of small, whether they are on the giving or receiving end, play a significant role in the boarders' lives.

A couple of foster families we visited are extremely assertive with respect to the inclusion of their patients: they decline invitations to happenings, receptions and dinners if their patients are not sincerely welcome. Furthermore, they adhere to this principle even when the parties take place outside Geel, on the initiative of non-Geelians. Again, this kind of behaviour is not prescribed by the OPZ. The Hospital is more than willing to look after the patients for one or two days when the foster parents are otherwise engaged. Nobody is coerced, not even morally, to share most aspects of their life with their guest. Needless to say, it does distinguish them when they do.

Many families are used to taking their patients along to the yearly market day or fancy fair, if the patients can physically manage. Families also attend sport happenings in which their patients participate, like fishing contests or tennis matches. In addition, they take part in the yearly barbecue where families and guests mix, eat together and dance. Every five years, foster parents, boarders and numerous other citizens of Geel march in the procession of Saint Dimpna in which all participants wear "historical" dress. At this occasion, they all get mixed, and, except in a few cases, patients cannot be distinguished from the rest.

Maintaining an inner circle

It is widely accepted, however, that not every single piece of information is shared with the patient. Certain issues, "family secrets" or other confidential matters are kept from him/her. In every foster family, an inner circle does exist in which the patient does not partake. This is considered sound practice. In this respect "a patient always remains a patient"—to quote one of the nurses—inclusion is never 100%. The inner circle is even considered an essential element of the system of foster care: some social distance is required between the foster family and its patient.

Keeping distance and staying in control

This phenomenon of claiming distance is related to another rule of thumb: "foster parents must be in charge." It is deemed absolutely wrong to spoil the patient or to even give the impression that anything goes. The foster parent is the one in charge. In most cases, it is the foster mother who assumes this role, the system being overwhelmingly *matrifocal*. Anyway, someone in the foster family must regularly make clear that he or she is in control. If not, the tradition warns, the patient will take over and dominate the household.

Normal versus abnormal

In the local subculture, the moral right to stay in command is based on what is considered the solid fact that foster parents are able to draw on all their mental resources, while the patients are not. "They are not brought to Geel because or their sweaty feet!", was a comment we heard several times. To be mentally handicapped, unbalanced or disturbed is not considered equivalent to being normal. In that respect, foster parents do distance themselves from their patients, especially when talking to mental-health professionals. There is some conspiracy in the discourse between a "normal" outsider and the foster parents, a we-feeling in which the patient does not participate. We were never confronted with the idea that the world of the so-called normal people is full of madness too. The "philosophy" which professes that the gap between normal and abnormal is merely an arbitrary "construct" does not go down too well. In the circles of foster care, a sharp line is drawn between "normal" and "abnormal". This kind of thinking doesn't seem to stand in the way of tolerance. Quite to the contrary: one is willing to take a lot because the patients are not in Geel because of "sweaty feet".

The use of physical force

In some cases and at given times, distance and moral authority may not suffice. We have noted quite a number of stories on how, in the past, the use of physical force was part of the system. One sometimes had to physically restrain somebody. "To grab him" is a common expression. The foster family had to overpower aggressive patients during their fits. In recent decades and the last few years in particular, medication has significantly improved. As a consequence, physical force is no longer required. It is now considered a thing of the past. Until the middle of the 19th century chains and leather straps were used in Geel.

> *An elderly foster father, age 72, told us that he had "to grab" a patient once when the latter made a move to knock another family member on the head with a chair. This incident made such an impression on the patient, he never forgot it.*

> *Another foster parent related full of humour, how one of the guests at her parental home had to be physically restrained from time to time. Oddly enough the person in charge was not the father, nor one of the brothers, but one of the older girls, even though the rebellious guest was a man. The girl used to really fight and floor him, to finally sit on top of him. The guest called himself a communist, and referred to his enemy as "the Germans". Once the young woman had floored him, he used to capitulate proclaiming: "Yet again the communist have lost the battle and the Germans have won the war!"*

> *Some patients, muscular men mostly, never surrendered, not even when the entire family and the neighbours teamed up. In those cases a task force of four "hospital guards" was called in. These professional fighters usually managed to restrain the patient and take him to hospital. A given patient, a real fighter, used to challenge all males within his reach and only gave in to the Colony squad provided they all showed up. Surrendering to a limited delegation of two or three was definitely beneath him.*

The general attitude towards the use of physical force has changed dramatically over the years. It is no longer tolerated by the inhabitants of Geel.

> *When, recently, a district nurse was alarmed in the middle of the night that a female patient had turned violent, he hastened to the family's house and made a huge effort to force the patient into his car in order to take her to hospital. The guest, however, escaped and hid under the nurse's car. When he tried to drag her out from under the car, "she screamed her head off." Instead of helping the nurse, as they used to do in*

former times, the neighbours phoned the OPZ to complain, that a male nurse had abused a female patient on the street in the middle of the night.

Readmitting a patient to hospital
When a patient becomes very difficult and makes life impossible, the foster parent might warn the former that he is going to talk to the district nurse. A menace, that the OPZ may step in can work miracles. To be forced "to go back to the Colony (In-patient Care)" is generally perceived of as a true punishment. If the patient remains stubborn, is unable to change his/her behaviour or loses control, the menace is carried out. In this sense, the In-patient Care Unit has become an essential part of the system. From their side, the foster parents feel reassured that they can rely on help 24 hours a day. There is always support, they are never left to their own devices.

Accepting inherent limitations

A family we visited some 30 years ago still hosts the same patient, Pierre. For more than 40 years now, Pierre has been pilfering women's lingerie wherever and whenever he can find it: in his neighbours' gardens, elsewhere in Geel, and even in neighbouring villages. Surprisingly perhaps, Pierre behaves quite normally in all other domains. His foster parents have tried everything within their means to tackle Pierre's peculiar form of kleptomania, but to no avail. Pierre's habit has somewhat mellowed in recent years since he has more pocket money to buy a few precious pieces of women's underwear. Once in while, however, the urge is still too big to resist.

Just like Pierre's foster parents, others hit "a concrete wall" at a given point. They face the limit of their influence and power. They must be prepared to lose the battle as the practices and habits of their patients reign supreme.

An elderly patient who turned into a kind of beloved grandmother to the numerous grandchildren of her foster parents is another such example. "The children and the grandchildren absolutely adore her!", the foster parents affirm. The patient, however, wets herself when she is at home during the day. Remarkably, she never does so at night nor when she is on a visit, nor when she leaves on day-trips. A thorough physiological and neurological examination turned out negative: no deficiencies could be found. The ailment necessitates a daily bath. The patient, who is heavily overweight, refuses to collaborate, thus causing considerable strain to her foster parents who need to haul her out of the tub every single day. Nobody and nothing has been able to bring about change.

The affective bond
Social integration and steady authority are necessary components of the system. But things are only really running smoothly when a mutual emotional bond has developed: "It warms the bones," as one of the foster mothers states. Foster parents, especially foster mothers, are able to give much love and affection, but expect some response from their patient. It is striking that so many foster mothers compare patients with children, often young children. They state that they usually receive a lot in return, and that the patients' affection is true, genuine, not fake. Their loyalty is another redeeming feature: "Our own children leave us when they

get married; this one stays with us forever!" Dozens of foster parents spontaneously mention that they couldn't miss their guest; that the house is empty when their guest is on holiday; or that their boarder cries for joy when he embraces them upon returning home. A foster father told us in the presence of his wife that the family would keep its two male patients, even if the OPZ were to stop paying the allowance. Very often—and this is repeatedly stated by numerous foster parents—emotional attachment and signs of loyalty are what they do it for really.

> *A foster mother of 84 related that one of her former guests died from brain cancer. At the end, he was no longer able to speak, but a few hours before he died he had pressed her hand, whispering: "Have been good to me!" The elderly lady couldn't hold back her tears when she told this story.*
>
> *A foster father of 84 and a foster mother of 82, who still host two male patients, reminisced about their former patient Lowie, who passed away at the age of 64: "Lowie did so much for our children! No parent will do as much for his own!" Lowie always prepared their lunchboxes and used to shine their shoes. When one of the sons of the family, Georges, joined the army, Lowie got depressed. Although he had never travelled before, he accompanied the recruit to his barracks at the town of Turnhout. Both parents were strongly moved while telling Lowie's story. They clearly idealized Lowie and cherished his warm and kind disposition.*

Again and again foster parents stress, that their patients care a lot about their "mother" and "father". They repeatedly ask how things are going when a member of the family is ill. Of course, this concern has also to do with the fear of losing a parent and of the consequences this entails. The patients' feelings may not be entirely altruistic but are genuine, all the same. Several foster parents told us spontaneously that they clean the tomb of their deceased guest prior to All Saints and decorate it with flowers, just like they do for the rest of the family.

In some cases true friendship develops, and a kind of almost symmetric confidentiality evolves between the foster parent—mostly the foster mother—and the boarder.

> *The two "sisters" (described in case 14 supra) interact like two relatives, telling each other in the evening about their experiences of the day.*
>
> *In another case, X and Y are quite different as far as their mental capacity is concerned, but every week they go out like friends. They are the same age and have grown up together.*
>
> *Or yet another case: "When he is down, I talk to him and cheer him up, and then he is happy again," says a 70-year-old foster mother about her 64-year-old "son" who tends to get depressed.*

If this reciprocal emotional bond which reinforces social inclusion is not present, the relationship becomes problematic. In about 10 cases out of 108, we noticed that the relationship was bound to fail because any form of rapport was missing. A foster family put it very clearly: "He was a nice young man, but he was not able to accept what he was offered by the other members of the family. We had to let him go." Lots of foster parents remarked that the "new types" of patients the OPZ has introduced into the system—some of them former alcohol or drug addicts—will never be accepted in Geel. If no emotional ties develop, other inconveniences which are usually disregarded in a harmonious relationship come to the fore and turn into obstacles one is no longer willing to overcome. When, on the contrary, a mutual warm relationship evolves, foster parents are prepared to go to great lengths to accommodate their guests.

Boarders and children: an additional bond
All foster parents who have children and grandchildren—and that's basically all of them—consider the relationship between their guests and the kids of prime importance. In most cases they have an excellent relationship. Many patients occasionally join the young children or grandchildren when they are playing. If they are able to, they help them with their school work. Many patients like to horse around with the children and gladly accept being "mistreated", "tortured" or teased by them. "They are really attracted to each other," says one foster mother. In a few cases we came across, no rapport between the guest and the foster parents' young children or grandchildren had developed.

> *A female patient in her 50s threatened to crush the toys of the grandson if he left them scattered all over the place one more time. This threat was reason enough for the foster parent to send the patient back to the Hospital.*
>
> *In two other cases the young mothers felt uncomfortable because the patient was not showing any interest in the children, and no healthy, open relationship had developed. The patients' attitude had stayed amorphous or unmarked. In both cases the guest was sent back to the OPZ.*

A cordial and open relationship between the patients and the children and grandchildren of the house constitutes an additional bond. In former days, when traffic in Geel was neither congested nor dangerous, quite a number of patients used to take the children to school and pick them up later. Even today a few patients do this.

> *Most children from his class think that the kind old lady who accompanies Ronny to school, is one of his grandmothers. They call her "grandma Zoë". Actually, Zoë is a patient who lives with Ronny's grandmother.*

Dozens of foster parents we visited told us that they and their children were as good as raised by boarders. Time and again they stressed how remarkably well patients and children get along. It boils down to this: if patients wish to attach, they are never discouraged by the foster parents. Once a click has been made, the patient will never be sent back to the OPZ, not even when his/her behaviour goes downhill with age. Once the children and grandchildren have attached to the guest, it is virtually impossible to send him/her away.

Although some negative images of the past may emerge from time to time, memories about "the lads from the Colony" are overwhelmingly positive. The explanation for this is perfectly simple. The relationship between the patients and the children and grandchildren tends to be pleasant everywhere, for the obvious reason that patients who are rude or insensitive to children are dismissed early on. A positive selection takes place. This selection also prevailed in the past, as was observed by scholars in the 19th century (cf. *Chapter I*). Patients walk and soothe babies, hold toddlers in their laps, and so on. This basic rapport between boarders and children seems to be an essential part of the system. Adult Geelians who have been raised by, or in the company of kind and bonding patients may be more inclined and better prepared to become foster parents than outsiders. Importantly, they may not see the presence of a patient in their house as threatening or disturbing. Many prejudices that are very much alive in the world at large are not found with Geelians who have been raised in the presence of mental patients. Remarkably, the idea that the presence of people with mental disabilities or impairments might be damaging to children hadn't occurred to anybody we met.

The families of origin

As was revealed in the case studies, contacts with the families of origin are diverse to say the least. Only a small minority of foster parents and patients are actively trying to keep in touch with the patient's relatives. The overwhelming majority of foster parents and guests, however, adopt a passive attitude. If family members call, they are kindly received. We met only two families out of 108 where relatives are no longer welcome: in the first case, the visitor was a prostitute trying to get hold of her sister's money; in the second, the language and conversation of the visitors were deemed "immoral" by the foster parents. In none of the 108 cases we visited, the OPZ planned to send the patient back to her family of origin. The patients were not deemed fit to return for mental, social and/or psychodynamic reasons. But mostly, the question did not even arise, because the relatives were no longer alive or available. However, a limited number of patients do get in touch with their relatives once or several times a year:

> *Joseph visits his mother who lives in a home for the elderly in another town of Flanders several days per month, by train. She used to visit her son in Geel very frequently when she was still in good health. Roles changed when the mother was no longer able to travel.*
>
> *Pierre's parents are wealthy. They often come by, paying the bills of their spendthrift son.*
>
> *Marie-Paule's parents pick her up several times a year for a day-trip. In their tiny apartment, they have no room to keep her overnight.*
>
> *Francine is visited by one of her brothers and his entire family three times a year.*
>
> *Maurice's sister is a missionary living on another continent. She always visits her brother on the very day she returns to Belgium. Maurice's two co-boarders stressed this remarkable sisterly love.*

We only met one family of origin that encouraged, prepared and monitored the patient's return home.

> *Jacques was a young man from a wealthy family. His relatives visited every week or more. Jacques stayed in Geel incognito. His mental health improved considerably*

allowing him to return home. Jacques got married and became a caring family father with a full-time job. Jacques still visits his former foster parents. "I owe you everything!", he keeps repeating.

But in most cases the family context is either lacking or unfit to offer a decent home. In order to fully respect privacy, we keep the following data vague. The names are pseudonyms. We only select a few cases from a long list.

Yvette has been sexually abused in her family when she was a child. Her husband has committed incest with one of her daughters. Her mother died when she was very young. The future of all of her children seems very problematic.

Jean-Pierre is not able to remember who his parents were. He had been living with "the brothers" (members of a religious congregation) since he was very little. He told us that he was ordered to undress again and again by one of the brothers who then "hung him from the wall". The federal police picked up Jean-Pierre at the brothers' and brought him to another institution.

One day Michel received the visit of a mother whom he had barely met. She was accompanied by the mayor of her village and came to check if her son could come and live with her. What she really wanted, however, was his money and part of the salary he might earn. Michel refused to meet her after that incident.

Marie-Louise's mother visited regularly. She died a long time ago. Marie-Louise came from a well-to-do family and inherited a considerable sum of money. When a few years ago she was taken to the local general hospital to undergo major surgery, her relatives were informed. These distant relatives, who had never bothered to visit before, called at the hospital and seemed disappointed when they learned that surgery had been successful and Marie-Louise had survived. They have never been heard of since. Marie-Louise decided to make her foster parents her sole heirs.

Yvonne's mother was a prostitute. Her father was "employed" in the same branch, and Yvonne was encouraged by her own mother to join "the business". She later married. Her daughter was born into that marriage and still visits her mother from time to time. Yvonne has no contact with her son who was probably born out of wedlock.

Jeanne's parents were both alcoholics. She herself became addicted at a very young age. At a very tender age, she was taken down to the cellar and sexually abused by a visitor. She hates her family and everything that reminds her of them.

For all his long years in Geel, Hector was visited by his daughter, a university graduate, only once, i.e., after his other daughter had died in a car accident. Hector hasn't heard from her since.

These days, when new patients enter the programme, the OPZ social workers actively pursue the matter of family contacts. Clients tend to stay in their own region, so contact is usually possible. At all times, the needs and wishes of the clients involved prevail and determine which line of action is taken vis-à-vis the biological family.

Lasting loyalty
It is an unspoken but highly respected ethical rule of the Geel tradition, that children, if possible, take over their parents' patient(s) when their parents are no longer in a position to provide care or pass away. A boarder who is fully integrated in the family is considered a member of the household and "is not sent away", even though there is no contract that states as much.

Reversal of roles
During our interviews, doctors, nurses as well as foster families pointed out a rather remarkable development: quite a few boarders have reversed roles of care giver and receiver of care. Having lived in a family for a long time, some take on the care of their aging foster parents as they grow old and feeble. Because of their sense of responsibility, the elderly can stay at home and are spared living in a retirement home. The patients do household chores, keep their parents company and help them cope with their physical disabilities. The erstwhile patient thus becomes a full-fledged care giver.

Relationship between the guest and the community: social integration in a broader social context (based on Roosens 1979a)

Co-varying with the degree of intimacy and intensity of the interaction between the guest and the Geelian(s) the following patterns emerge: On streets and public places recognition of the client is expressed through neutral, regular behaviour of the Geelian. The normal/abnormal (or deviant) boundary and the superiority of the normal vs. abnormal only emerge when the client's behaviour noticeably deviates. In that event, the Geelian will intervene and try to control the situation, be it directly or indirectly. In cafés and restaurants, Geelians will switch to "joking relations" when clients deviate: they "recognize" the boarders, listen and talk to them, but do stop taking them seriously, and show it. Joking relations are a way to preserve the boundary between normal and abnormal, and to underscore the superiority of the normal.

The degree of a guest's social integration in the larger Geel community needs to be further qualified. As agriculture and horticulture sharply declined and the guests' employment in this area basically evaporated, the OPZ started organizing work in workshops on its premises. It also introduced its own sports club and set up travel for its clients (cf. *Chapter II*). This is a clear sign that the overwhelming majority of the boarders could not be absorbed in the local labour market. Regular sport facilities and holidays were not readily accessible either. Yet another restriction is situated at macro level: not all people with serious mental problems are admitted to the foster care programme. Aggressive persons, arsonists, etc. are excluded. Moreover, it is unclear how big the impact of the mental health team is on the level of integration.

From what precedes, we would like to conclude that, whatever the remarkable Geelian goodwill, *total* social equivalence between a guest and a Geelian cannot be found. *Total* integra-

Household chores
(Photo D. Theys)

tion or *total* social absorption remains an illusion and is not brought about. Will "normal" and "abnormal" ever really merge? Should they merge, indeed? What makes Geel remarkable is not the blurring of the normal/abnormal boundary, but the recognition of the clients' human dignity to the extent that life in a family and wider community is given an honest chance every single day.

| Conclusion |

Geel's own brand of organically grown rehabilitation

In our analysis we have demonstrated that Geel has successfully rehabilitated psychiatric patients all along (cf. *Chapter I*). By the middle of the 19th century Geel had already met lots of targets set by present-day scholars and policymakers, who invested a lot of time and energy in the process. Lots of characteristics, which literature associates with successful rehabilitation (Lamb and Bachrach 2001; van Weeghel et al. 2005), are inherent in the Geel approach (cf. *Chapter IV*). Geel is a good example of organically grown rehabilitation, rehabilitation *avant la lettre*. It is not perfect a system, but it does offer people a natural and dignified life in the community.

Stigma

Good community care may be highly recommended but it is not easy to achieve. (Van Weeghel[10] as reported in Van de Walle 2005:32). Stigma is a huge problem; both stigma by others and self-stigma. Contemporary national and international public services, as well as volunteer organizations, try to tackle the stigma that sets people with mental problems apart or keeps them at a distance. They do so with media campaigns, by working on pupils and students in schools, by discussions in the media. With varying success. Studies conclude that the prejudices that are supposedly at the root of the unsatisfactory level of integration of the mentally ill are hard to eradicate (Corrigan 2004, Warner 2005). Contact is probably the most successful antistigma strategy. Why this is so, is described in Couture & Penn (2003). The gist of it is, that contact between people with and without psychiatric limitations has a more positive effect if both parties have equal status; they both elect to have contact; contacts are characterised by co-operation and involve some degree of trust; it concerns contacts that deviate to some extent from the stereotype.

In Geel, contacts between patients and regular citizens, whether they are foster families or not, basically correspond to these guidelines. Contacts come natural. We are not claiming here there is no stigma in Geel. One needs extensive research to find out which types of stigma are present, and to what extent. It is clear, however, that the community is supportive and tolerant of people who are different and/or display "weird" behaviour. In Geel, one does not need contrived actions and events to bridge the gap between the two groups. Because patients are accepted as they are, their self-stigma is likely to be positively influenced in the long term as well[11].

10 Based on a study by Van Hoof et al. (2004).

11 Evidently, this is just an assumption based on our own perception. As is the case for stigma by others, one needs to thoroughly research these issues.

Social integration, "balanced care" and long-term support

But there is more. As for social integration, "balanced care" and (very) long-term support, Geel performs better than many other organizations or organization forms; that is, if one adopts as reference point the research report drawn up by Bauduin, McCullogh en Liégeois, *Good care in the community: Ethical aspects of deinstitutionalisation in mental health care* (2002).

Since the sixties health policies in the US, the wider Anglo-Saxon world and several European countries have been geared towards deinstitutionalisation of psychiatric care. New terms and phrases such as "psychiatric rehabilitation", "community psychiatry", "social integration of people with severe psychiatric disorders" were introduced. Recent research in the Netherlands, Belgium, the UK, Italy and Greece has lead prominent researchers to the following conclusions (Bauduin et al. 2002):

First, in the countries involved in this particular study, policymakers aimed at closing as many psychiatric institutions "of the old type" as possible. They also aimed at reducing the number of hospital beds available to patients with long-term problems to a strict minimum. Results were staggering: in the UK 142,000 beds were available in 1960; in the 90s this number had dwindled to 5,000. In Italy one went from 60,000 in 1978 to 2,500 in 1998. In Greece the capacity was halved: the total number dropped from 8,000 in 1980 to 4,500 in 1998. In the Netherlands the total number has hardly changed, but the intention still exists to decommission beds. In Belgium the number of beds went down by 30% between 1980 en 1995. This period is generally described as the "Decline of the Asylum" (WHO 2006).

Second, in these countries innovative services were established to replace the traditional asylums. In the UK, for example, services were set up—be it too few—to offer psychiatric patients protection, intensive care and social support in the community. In Italy the number of mental health service centres soared from 226 in 1978 to 4,000 in 1998. In Greece new services got established, but only in the 80s. In the Netherlands, sheltered accommodation and support services doubled between 1980 and 1995. In Belgium the number of community mental health centres increased by 25%. In all of these countries community care was actively promoted as the rehabilitation model "par excellence". But as the WHO label for this period, i.e., "Balanced Care" (2006), suggests, providing a range of community-based services within local settings is an excellent idea, provided there is sufficient support by a hospital.

The right balance is the key. In Geel that balance has been well-guarded since the establishment of the Hospital in 1851. In several other countries, however, one failed to recognize the importance of a decently funded in-patient facility in one's enthusiasm to get everybody out in the community, regardless of the severity of one's illness.

Third, without a doubt, outcomes are good:

> *The substantial changes in mental health care, the legal reinforcement of the patient's position, and the improvement of the professional-client relationship have resulted in important benefits for the majority of people with mental health problems. They experience more freedom, in that they have more options and can lead*

> *more 'normal' lives. They have more social roles up to them other than that of being mentally ill and have more opportunities to choose their own course of recovery from psychiatric problems. They also have more activities during the day, thanks to more active rehabilitation programmes. In short, they enjoy more independence, autonomy and privacy* (Bauduin et al. 2002: 15).

Fourth, positive as those outcomes might be, the new approach does fall short in a number of ways. One does arrive at supporting, and, if necessary, protecting people with enduring psychiatric illnesses, but as for their integration in the social network of the community they live in, results are sooner disappointing. Social integration appears to be the most elusive goal in all countries involved in the study.

Finally, sustaining support over very long periods of time remains problematic:

> *To the detriment of patients, neither the community, nor in many cases the professionals, have been ready to accept the need for long-term support from community and professional resources* (Bauduin et al. 2002: 7).

Geel is a strong concept on both accounts: both social integration and long-term care are at its core. As amply demonstrated in the case analysis, social inclusion is a rule of thumb in the Geel system. The guests' inclusion in the family has been observed by scores of experts and commentators since the middle of the 19th century. Continuity of care is a forte too: guests often remain in the same family and are passed on from generation to generation. As described above, children feel responsible for their parents' guests and offer them a home after the latter have passed on.

This brings us to the conclusion that psychiatric foster care in Geel successfully rehabilitates. Integration is not contrived. It is natural and spontaneous. People with severe mental disabilities are welcome in Geel. They get the time to come into their own and get established in the community. Time is Geel's ally.

As for the future, one can only say that rehabilitation is in Geel's "cultural gene pool". It is there to stay.

Pressing issues

Contemporary psychiatric foster care in Geel is not simply a remnant of the Middle Ages. The system has undergone at least two marked transformations. A first time in the middle of the 19th century, when Geel was taken over by the state which immediately introduced medical supervision. And a second time, in the last 40 forty years, as the impact of professionals gradually increased. Presently, the OPZ provides work, leisure and activities to an ever-rising number of patients. During the day, over 50% of patients are under the supervision of paramedical staff; they are not at home. Staff members have thus taken over part of what used to be the job of foster parents. Moreover, patients reside on and off in the in-patient facility, which is an integral part of the foster care system these days. Given these facts, one cannot but conclude that Geel has become a two-layered system. A number of key elements of the traditional system have remained intact, however: maximal kin-like inclusion and integration of the patient; the kindness of the broader social context in Geel; the acceptance of a patient's inherent limitations; the strong bond between boarders and foster families; the resilient mutual loyalty; and the entrenched responsibility of the next generation towards the boarders. All these are strong markers.

This remarkable foster family care system may well be under threat if the number of new patients and foster families is not stabilized at some point in the near future. Active intervention is needed on several fronts: the management needs to fine-tune the system; to relate to, and support the families and their guests as best it can. A solid communication strategy needs to be in place to explain the system both to the general public and professionals. Research, possibly with international scope, is needed to understand and uncover the "mechanisms", the healing effects of this form of community care. Good relations need to be developed with Geel and the surrounding communities; avenues need to be explored to start up psychiatric foster care elsewhere in Flanders, not as an isolated programme but as an integral part of a larger community care programme, geared towards long-term help. The programme needs to continuously reinvent itself, provide a mixed portfolio of services and consider other target groups (adolescents, single mothers with child, geriatric patients, etc.).

According to the WHO HEN report (2006: 6)[12], there is a great shortage of specialized outpatient facilities for specific disorders or patient groups. Foster care means patients can lead a dignified and meaningful life; so, the more people get access to this form of community care, the better.

Last but not least, the management needs to lobby the government for a fair and sustainable funding mechanism, so that it can both continue to provide good quality care and adequately compensate and recruit foster families. In some countries, like France, Italy and the UK, foster families even get an official contract which means they are recognized for what they do. They accrue pension rights, are entitled to social security benefits, holiday money, etc. It may take the Belgian authorities a while to change their approach and get this organized, but it would most certainly be a clear signal, that it fully appreciates its heritage and sees fostering of psychiatric patients as a valid and valuable alternative to other forms of community care and institutionalization. At this point, kind words of support no longer do; it is action that is required, sooner rather than later.

12 HEN: Health Evidence Network

References

Aluffi, G. (2005) Psychiatric reform and territorialization of the mental health services in Italy: The foster family care project of the university mental health dept. In *Piemonte.* Talk at the *Congress Balanced Care*, Geel.

Bachrach, L. (2000) Note.

Bogaerts, W. (1999) Internal document.

Bogaerts, W. (2006) Internal document.

Bauduin, D., McCulloch, A., Liégeois, A. (2002) *Good care in the community: Ethical aspects of deinstitutionalisation in mental health care.* Utrecht: Netherlands Institute of Mental Health and Addiction. Trimbos-instituut.

Brierre de Boismont, A. (1852) Une visite à la colonie de Geel en 1846. *Annales Médico-Psychologiques*, 1852 Vol. 4 (2): 520-546.

Carmichael McIntosh, W. (1862) Notes on asylums and the insane in France and Belgium. *The Journal of Mental Science*, April 1862 Vol. VIII(40): 1-36.

Corrigan, P. (2004) Target-specific stigma change: A strategy for impacting mental illness stigma. *Psychiatric Rehabilitation Journal*, Fall 2004 Vol. 28(2): 113-121.

Couture, S. & Penn, D. (2003) Interpersonal contact and the stigma of mental illness: A review of the literature. *Journal of Mental Health*, 12(3): 291-305.

Curry, R. and Lally, R. (2005) Moving on: Services to promote greater quality of life and independence. Talk at the *Congress Balanced Care*, Geel.

De Bont, M. (1976) De Heilige Dimpna en de Geelse gezinsverpleging. In *Geel, van gisteren tot morgen.* Lions Mol-Geel: 467-476.

De Bont, M. (1989) "The Geel Question". De gezinsverpleging in de internationale belangstelling (1821-1902). In *Geel, de stad der simpelen.* Jaarboek 26 - 1989 van de Vrijheid en het Land van Geel. Geel: Geels Geschiedkundig Genootschap: 159-174.

Discussion sur la colonisation des aliénés (1862). *Annales Médico-Psychologiques*, 1862 Vol. 8 (3): 683-689.

DSM-IV. Lisse: Swets & Zeitlinger, 1997.

Duval, J. (1867) *Geel ou une colonie d'aliénés.* Paris.

Eynikel, H. (1971a) *De uitbreiding en beoordeling van de gezinsverpleging van geesteszieken. Uitstraling van het Schotse en Geelse systeem (1850-1970). (Eindverhandeling aangeboden tot het bekomen van de graad van licentiaat in de Moderne Geschiedenis door Hilde Eynikel).* Louvain: 1971 (typescript).

Eynikel, H. (1971b) Geel, bakermat van de gezinsverpleging. *Annalen van de Belgische Vereniging voor Hospitaalgeschiedenis*, 1971, IX: 113-123.

Foreign psychological literature (1860) On the management of the insane in Belgium. By Dr. J. Parigot. *Journal of Psychological, Medical and Mental Pathology*, 1860 Vol. XIII: 600-603.

Godemont, M. (2000) Geel as a model. In: *Proceedings Geel 2000*: 7-13.

Held, T. (2005) Foster family care and the changing paradigms of social psychiatry. Talk at the *Congress Balanced Care*, Geel.

Koyen, M. H. (1973) Gezinsverpleging van geesteszieken te Geel tot het einde van de 18de eeuw. In *Jaarboek van de Vrijheid en het Land van Geel*, dl. 12.

Lamb, R. and Bachrach, L. (2001) Some perspectives on deinstitutionalization. *Psychiatric Services*, August 2001 (52):1039-1045.

Loiseau, J. (1862a) Rapport de M. Jules Falret, au nom de la Commission de Geel. *Annales Médico-Psychologiques*, 1862 (3): 138-170.

Loiseau, J. (1862b) Report on Geel by the Commission of the Medico-Psychological Society of Paris, read at the sitting of the Society, December 30th, 1861. *Journal of Mental Science*, 1862 Vol. 8: 102-118.

Moreau (de Tours), J. (1845) Lettres médicales sur la colonisation de Geel. *Annales Médico-Psychologiques*, 1845: 89-112, 264-279.

Parigot, J. (1863) The Geel question: From an American point of vue. *Journal of Insanity*, January 1863: 332-354.

Piat, M. (2005), Partnership between foster home care givers and the Health and Social Service Network. Talk at the *Congress Balanced Care*, Geel.

Pieters, G. & Peuskens, J. (eds.) (1995) Rehabilitatie van de chronische psychiatrische patiënt. Louvain/Apeldoorn: Garant.

Roosens, E. (1977) *Geel, een unicum in de psychiatrie. Mentale patiënten in de gemeenschap.* Antwerp/Amsterdam: De Nederlandsche Boekhandel.

Roosens, E. (1979a) *Mental patients in town life: Geel—Europe's first therapeutic community*. Beverly Hills/London: Sage Publications.

Roosens, E. (1979b) *Des fous dans la ville? Geel et sa thérapie séculaire.* Paris: Presses universitaires de France.

Roosens, E. (1982) *Geel. No machi nohitobito*. Tokyo: Japanese Society of Psychiatry.

Roosens, E; (1983) *Psychisch Kranke unter uns. Geel: Eine Stadt integriert seelische Kranke in ihre Gemeinschaft*. Stuttgart: Hippokrates Verlag.

Roosens, E. (2001) *Dansen met de maan. Gezinsverpleging in Geel.* Louvain: Uitgeverij Van Halewyck.

Sano, F. (1903) *Congrès international de l'assistance des aliénés et spécialement de leur assistance familiale. (Tenu à Anvers du 1 au 7 septembre 1902). Rapports et compte-rendu des séances*. Antwerp: De Nederlandsche Boekhandel, 1902.

Sibbald, J. (1861) The cottage system and Geel. *Journal of Mental Science*, 1861, Vol. 7(37): 31-61.

Van de Walle, L. (2005) Vernieuwende visies op psychiatrische rehabilitatie: Congress Balanced Care. *Passage*, 2005, 2: 31-35.

van Hoof, F., Geelen, K., van Rooijen, S., van Weeghel, J. (2004). *Meedoen. Maatschappelijke ondersteuning van mensen met psychische handicaps*. Utrecht: Trimbosreeks, 2004-5.

van Weeghel, J., Van Audenhove, Ch., Garanis-Papadatos, T., Liégeois, A., McCulloch, A., Muijen, M., Norcio, B., Ploumbidis, D. and Bauduin, D. (2005) The components of good community care for people with severe mental illnesses: Views of stakeholders in five European countries. *Psychiatric Rehabilitation Journal*, Winter 2005, Vol. 28(3): 274-281.

Veraghtert, K. (1969) De overheid en de Geelse gezinsverpleging (1660-1860). *Annalen van de Belgische Vereniging voor Hospitaalgeschiedenis*, 1969, VII: 113-127.

Veraghtert, K. (1971) De Geelse gezinsverpleging als regionale welvaartsfactor (1795-1860). *Bijdragen tot de geschiedenis,* 1971: 3-30.

Veraghtert, K. (1972) De krankzinnigenverpleging te Geel (1795-1860). In *Jaarboek van de Vrijheid en het Land van Geel*, 1972, dl. 11: 1-148.

Veraghtert, K. (1976) Niet-gepubliceerde bijdrage tot het Internationaal Symposium over Gezinsverpleging voor Geesteszieken. Geel.

Veraghtert, K. (1976) Geel: nationaal en internationaal verplegingsoord. In *Geel van gisteren tot morgen*. Lions Mol-Geel: 492-507.

Warner, R. (2005) Local projects of the World Psychiatric Association Programme to reduce stigma and discrimination. *Psychiatric Services*, May 2005 Vol. 56(5): 570-575.

Webster, J. (1857) Notes on Belgian lunatic asylums, including the insane Colony of Geel. *Journal of Psychological, Medical and Mental Pathology*, 1857, X: 209-247.

Willers Jessen (1860) Geel: Letter from Dr. Willers Jessen. *Journal of Psychological, Medical and Mental Pathology*, 1860 Vol. XIII: 612-613.

World Health Organization (2001) *World health report 2001: Mental health: New understanding, new hope*. Geneva (http://who.int/whr2001/2001/main/en, accessed July 13, 2003).

World Health Organization, Health Evidence Network (HEN) (2006). *The components of a balanced care mental health service* (http://www.euro.who.int/HEN/Synthe1sis/mental health/2006).

Index